LONGITUDE

To
my Swedish grandchildren
Jonatan and Miriam
may you find your way
in the world

LONGITUDE

A play by

ARNOLD WESKER

Based on the book 'Longitude' by Dava Sobel

Amber Lane Press

All rights whatsoever in this play are strictly reserved and application
for professional performance should be made before rehearsals begin to:
Nicky Lund, David Higham Associates
5-8 Lower John Street, Golden Square, London W1F 4HA
E-mail: nickylund@davidhigham.co.uk

Application for amateur performance should be made before rehearsals
begin to:
Arnold Wesker, Hay on Wye, Hereford, HR3 5RJ
E-mail: wesker@compuserve.com

No performance may be given unless a licence has been obtained.

First published in 2006 by
Amber Lane Press Ltd
Church Street, Charlbury, Oxon OX7 3PR
Telephone: 01608 810024
E-mail: info@amberlanepress.co.uk

Printed and bound by
Creative Print and Design Group, Harmondsworth and Ebbw Vale

Copyright © Arnold Wesker, 2005
The right of Arnold Wesker to be recognised as author of this work has
been asserted in accordance with the Copyright, Designs and Patents
Act, 1988

ISBN: 1 872868 40 1

CONDITIONS OF SALE
This book is sold subject to the condition that it shall not by way of
trade or otherwise, be lent, resold, hired out or otherwise circulated
without the publisher's prior consent in any form of binding or cover
other than that in which it is published and without a similar condition,
including this condition being imposed on the subsequent purchaser.

'Longitude – the Play' received its world premiere at Greenwich Theatre, London, on 10 October 2005. It was directed by Fiona Laird with the following cast:

JOHN HARRISON	Anthony O'Donnell
ELIZABETH HARRISON	Mossie Smith
WILLIAM HARRISON	Hadley Fraser
LORD EGMONT	Nick Tigg
LORD MORTON	Mark Meadows
REV. NEVIL MASKELYNE	Giles Taylor
COMMISSIONER	Kieran Hill
MARTIN FOLKES/SIR KENELM DIGBY/ THOMAS KING/GEORGE III	Dominic Marsh
DR EDMOND HALLEY/ WILLIAM LUDLAM/ DR DEMAINBRAY	Christopher Staines
GEORGE GRAHAM/ ROGER WILLS/ LARCUM KENDALL	James Thorne

Designer : Anthony Lamble
Music : Paul Englishby
Lighting Designer : Ian Scott
Sound designer: Neil Fulcher

I wish gratefully to acknowledge that the producers, Green and Lenagan, originally commissioned the writing of this adaptation.

About This Play and Its Production

Its feel is Hogarthian.
Its sweep is epic.
Its drive is story-telling.
Its staging convention is, let's say – loose.

The spirit is that of a group of actors who've come together to enact a story. One minute they're a character, the next a street trader crying out wares, the next they're part of a choir.

I see John Harrison's life as a series of body blows, and therefore the stage bristles with activity. Something is always happening – whether it's singing or celebration, bustling street-life or verbal conflict.

We are telling a story driven by genius and eccentricity at a time in England's history when science, medicine, engineering and manufacture are on the brink of bursting into the Industrial Revolution.

I have only occasionally indicated what the main characters maybe doing on stage while another action is taking place – John in his workshop, Elizabeth kneading dough and so on – but actions domestic or to do with work or in the form of street and tavern life will be devised by the director or actors themselves to keep the stage alive without being too fussy, too restless.

Above all, Harrison's is a constant and pervading presence throughout.

Setting

By 'Hogarthian' is meant multi-layered: streets, alleys, Georgian shop fronts with hanging boards, stone steps, railings . . .

Somewhere among it all are:

Church pews in a small Lincolnshire church
A church bell
Red Lion Square – Harrison's house showing main room, his workshop, Elizabeth's kitchen
Announcement platform
Greenwich Observatory
Graham's workshop
The Admiralty
A heaving ship's cabin on the H.M.S *Orford*
A London tavern
Richmond Observatory
Temporary observatory in Barbados
Ship's cabin

Characters

Nine actors will play seventeen parts. Must be able to sing.

John Harrison
Elizabeth Harrison
William Harrison – their son
Commissioner – reader of legal documents
Dr Edmond Halley – one of the Astronomers Royal
George Graham – clockmaker
Martin Folkes – President of the Royal Society
Roger Wills – master of the H.M.S. *Orford*
Sir Kenelm Digby – diplomat interested in alchemy and astrology
Rev. Nevil Maskelyne – one of the Astronomers Royal
Lord Morton
Lord Egmont
Thomas King – portrait artist
William Ludlam – mathematician, Fellow of St John's College, Cambridge.
George III
Dr Demainbray – Swiss tutor to George III, keeper of the Royal Observatory, Richmond
Larcum Kendall – clockmaker
Street traders and others (if available)

Possible allotment of parts

One actor to play:
Harrison
Elizabeth
William
Maskelyne
Commissioner, Folkes
Halley, Morton
Graham, Egmont
Ludlam, Kendall, George III
Digby, Wills, Thomas King, Demainbray

Notes

About dialect: I don't know the Lincolnshire dialect and so have only here and there hinted at a 'northern dialect'. The right, knowledgeable actors would no doubt change some of the dialogue to achieve the right lilt.

This published version differs from the performed version in that cuts and changes were made after the performance had settled and the alterations required became apparent.

Introduction to 'Longitude – the Play'

By 1714 so many lives and so much merchandise had been lost at sea because longitude could not be identified that Parliament was petitioned by merchants and sailors for something to be done about it.

A prize of £20,000 was offered to whoever solved the problem.

The problem of longitude was that it could only be identified either by tabulating the position of the moon and stars or by having a clock on board a ship. The stars option was considered the most likely solution because, as Sir Isaac Newton observed, the motion of the ship, the variation of heat and cold, wet and dry, and the differences of gravity made it unlikely that such a watch could ever be invented.

During that century a carpenter from Lincolnshire, John Harrison, defied the established experts and invented such a clock.

For various reasons Harrison was not awarded the full prize, and spent a cantankerous life fighting to be recognised and rewarded.

The play 'Longitude', based on the best-selling book by Dava Sobel, charts that cantankerous struggle of uneducated genius against the establishment.

The first two problems confronting the playwright who must adapt the story, told by a scientific journalist, into a play are period (eighteenth-century England) and dialogue. Sobel is a brilliant journalist of scientific matters, and she has researched her background meticulously. What her book could not contain, inevitably, was dialogue to help bring the characters to life on a stage. Nor is there a portrait of John Harrison's wife because little is known about her; likewise little is known of John Harrison's son, William.

What Sobel's book *does* provide for the playwright is a bibliography of rich source material. The sources she used to write her book I used to write the play. Instinct drew me to reach out to a life of John Harrison by Humphrey Quill (*John Harrison, Copley Medalist and the £20,000 Longitude Prize*) and John Harrison's own books and pamphlets.

Eighteenth-century English is not the most flowing prose. There is a certain tortuousness to its structure, it is a convoluted assembly over which the modern tongue trips when read aloud. Add to this that John Harrison's prose was excruciating, virtually a foreign language that I had to translate, and it will be understood how it was a lengthy and difficult process; but finally rewarding in that his personality came through, providing me with a quality of dialogue genuinely rooted in the man and his times.

The most helpful aspect of Quill's book was that he understood the drama of the conflict between John Harrison and the eighteenth-century scientific establishment, and thus was able to place himself inside Harrison's cantankerous head and the reasonable if mean-spirited minds of members of the Board of Longitude.

There is no doubt that Harrison earned and deserved the Longitude Prize, and that the Board kept shifting the goal posts. But on the one hand Harrison was prickly, combative, and undiplomatic; on the other the Board had a responsibility to ensure that no matter what genius was at work the product of that genius's mind had to lend itself to practical reproduction. Therein lay the conflict and the tension: the drama of uneducated genius pitting itself against the brilliant but arrogant minds of the scientific establishment that couldn't believe an uneducated man from up north could achieve what they had not.

The irony is that Harrison ended up receiving more money than the £20,000 prize offered by the Longitude Board. But it didn't come from the Board. King George III intervened and secured an award from Parliament for 'achievement'. This mollified Harrison but barely. He remained aggrieved that the full amount didn't come from the Board. He felt patronised.

I can see the kind of irascible curmudgeon Harrison must have been for those high and mighty Lords and Oxbridge professors whom he despised. He knew he was right. The English establishment has never been able to countenance such certitude. There must always, quite rightly, be room for doubt. Genius has difficulty accepting such a possibility, especially as 'doubt' has a price. Shakespeare phrased it succinctly in Sonnet 66: '*And right perfection wrongfully disgraced . . . And simple truth miscall'd simplicity/And captive good attending captain ill . . .*' Or, as Harrison warns his son:

> I know all about them as glory in the end of things, the passing of this and that. He's had his day, they say with sadness in their voice and glee in their dried up hearts. Expect no more from him. His days are ended, done! Well pass I won't and end I won't and more there is, and they can choke with glee for I've got oak and God and cleverness where they've got naught but three chins and a shiny arse. Oh, yes, I know such men. Beware of them, William lad. They'll drain joy from a nightingale, dampen your sun, and lay waste the best in you.

©Arnold Wesker, 2005

ACT ONE

Setting in shadow.

Sounds of:

A ticking clock.
A growing storm.
Timber shattering on rock.
Human voices in distress.

Over all this, out of the shadows, a woman's lamenting voice:

ELIZABETH: [*The Litany*] The *Association*, six hundred and fifty lives lost. The *Marigold*, five hundred and forty lives lost. The *Eagle*, four hundred and ninety lives lost. The *Romney*, four hundred and fifty lives lost . . .

Sound of CHOIR.

Lights.

Church Pews/Elizabeth's Kitchen/ The Bell

HARRISON *conducting.*

ELIZABETH *kneading dough.*

ELIZABETH: And then – four ships of Sir Clowdisley Shovell's fleet – scuttled. Nearly two thousand lives lost. An experienced commander but he steered four prized ships on to the rocks of the Scilly Isles. Why? How came this?

Pause.

Longitude! They couldn't find longitude. Thought they were where they weren't. Disaster upon disaster. Precious lives, precious cargo, precious trade, precious wars – lost. Shook the nation, and made Parliament sit up.

Singing continues.

So they had to pass an Act. In the reign of Queen Anne – the Longitude Act.

HARRISON: Sing out you weavers, sing out you smithies! Sing out you shoemakers, carpenters, ploughmen and boys. Sing out!

He joins them.

Distress dies away, leaving the singing.

And that's how I want us always to sing – basses in front, tenors in the pews behind, trebles behind them. And *facing* the congregation, not with your backs to them but facing.

The street life takes over.

Bustle. Music. Street cries.

HARRISON *pulls a church bell. He has just tuned it. He will strike it five times.*

ELIZABETH: What's shipwrecks got to do with singing, you're wondering? Nothing really, except it was one man thought about both. John Harrison –

Bell strike.

– carpenter and joiner –

Bell strike.

– tuner of bells –

Bell strike.

– choirmaster and mender of clocks –

Bell strike.

– helped change the world –

Bell strike.

– my husband.

'Town Crier' bell takes over.

HARRISON *moves to his workbench.*

COMMISSIONER, *ringing Town Crier's bell, mounts the Announcement Platform.*

COMMISSIONER: [*reading*] 'The Longitude Act. An Act for providing a public reward for such person or persons as shall discover the longitude at sea.'

ELIZABETH: It were such a problem that Parliament set up a committee to see what could be done. They asked advice from everyone. Even Sir Isaac Newton. It was his testimony got John going.

HARRISON: He's wrong! He's wrong! The old man is wrong!

ELIZABETH: Wrong about what, I asked him?

HARRISON: Newton says the best method to find longitude is by means of a clock that keeps time exactly but that no such clock can be made.

ELIZABETH: Why does Newton say that, I ask him?

HARRISON: Because –
ELIZABETH: – says my husband – who argued with everyone as I know to my cost –
HARRISON: – because of the motion of the ship, the changes between hot and cold, between wet and dry, and because the earth's gravity pulls differently in different parts of the world. But Sir Isaac is wrong. Such a clock *can* be made. I've made clocks that go accurately on land, I'll make one goes accurately at sea.
ELIZABETH: No arguing with a man who thinks he knows everything. Only my John didn't *think* he knew everything, he *knew* he knew everything.

Clanging bell.

Anyway, the committee recommended –
COMMISSIONER: [*reading*] '– that a reward of £20,000 be settled by Parliament upon such person or persons as shall discover a more certain and practicable method of asserting the longitude than any yet in practice, and that a Board of Longitude be set up to administer the award.'
ELIZABETH: Longitude! Don't ask me to explain it. John talked, explained, talked and explained and as soon as I thought I'd understood the science of it all I'd forget it.

Reaches for a sheet.

[*reading*] 'Mean time, which can be described as the time we use, is sundial time to which a correction known as the "equation of time" has been applied, thus causing the length of each day to be the same irrespective of the season.' Get your head round that. It's possible, I'm not saying it's not possible. But then – hold it! Repeat it! Explain it to someone else! Can you? I can't, but he could. He had a *natural* understanding of numbers and mechanical things, I just had his children. Well – that's not the whole truth. He was a natural mechanic but I was naturally wise, even though it's me who says it. I mean you can't help noticing you're wise alongside a body as unworldly as John Harrison.

Wipes her hands. Punches the cushion in his chair.

HARRISON: What were it about me?
ELIZABETH: They called thee strange, John Harrison.
HARRISON: 'Strange'? What were there strange? I made clocks. Taught myself to make clocks, what were strange about that?
ELIZABETH: You didn't accept payment.
HARRISON: In the beginning, no. I weren't easily content wi' what I'd done. Nowt strange about that.
ELIZABETH: They called thee obstinate, too.
HARRISON: 'Obstinate'? I saw wrong and said so and kept saying so and will always keep saying so. Wrong is wrong not obstinate. Honour is honour not obstinate. Justice is justice not obstinate. It were them were strange and obstinate. Priests and professors. Them!

Long, reflective pause.

Nay. Not them. Me. I didn't know my place. You're not born with rights, others must bestow them. Know your place, be humble, presume nothing. I learned none of that.

Pause.

Did I presume? I built something, changed men's fortunes – was that presumption?

Pause.

Nay. I presumed nothing. I earned. What I built *earned* me rights. I used my brain and brawn, and carved myself a place. Bestow me nothing, I said. I've earned. I wanted no bestowing, and told them so.

Pause.

And lost. Didn't know my place. Wasn't humble enough for them. Stupid man!

Pause.

Be fine when I'm long dead and gone and out of trouble's way, when they don't have my bluntness and gruffness and impatience and contempt of them grinding their ears. But alive? While I'm still around to argue back and disagree and write pamphlets 'gainst their mischievousness? Difficult! Presumptuous! Troublemaker!

Pause.

Bloody priests and professors.

ELIZABETH: You liked the Professor Halley.

Greenwich Observatory

HALLEY *and* HARRISON.

HARRISON: Y'see, metals expand, sir.
HALLEY: I know that.
HARRISON: But not at the same rate.
HALLEY: I know that, too.
HARRISON: And if you place brass alongside steel each expanding and contracting at different rates – as in this gridiron here – the pendulum stays the same length.

Pause.

Which means changing temperature won't distort the swing.

Pause.

Which means it'll keep time in cold climes and hot climes.
HALLEY: Congratulations, Mr Harrison. Impressive. Ingenious. But I am a man of the heavens.
HARRISON: And where are your heavens when storms come by day or mists by night?
HALLEY: I don't think you understand, sir.
HARRISON: [*He clowns.*] Help! Help! Lost! We're all lost.
HALLEY: This observatory was built specially, and my post as Astronomer Royal was created specially –
HARRISON: Help! Help!
HALLEY: And vast sums have been specially invested to chart the heavens, map the moon's movements and find longitude!
HARRISON: Lost! We're all lost!
HALLEY: Besides, sir, I know nothing of either mechanics or engineering.

HARRISON: Nothing?

HALLEY: Not enough to check your drawings and calculations. But – I know a clockmaker, George Graham –

HARRISON: Him?

HALLEY: You know him?

HARRISON: *Of* him.

HALLEY: A good man.

HARRISON: Could pirate my invention.

HALLEY: Not Graham.

HARRISON: I've learned to trust no man.

HALLEY: Well unlearn it or you'll go through life seeing the devil everywhere.

HARRISON: Which is where the devil is until us root him out.

HALLEY: Mr Harrison, sir, I must alert you, the Board of Longitude's members are astronomers, mathematicians, navigators. They will not welcome a mechanical solution over a lunar one. For them the only clock to be read is in the heavens. So take my advice and lower your guard a little. London is filled with some of the best minds of the age. George Graham is a man both of honesty and integrity, and the Board of Longitude just will not bother to meet you without his approval of your plans.

The streets come alive.

Bustle. Music. Street cries.

Graham's Workshop

HARRISON: Mr Graham?

GRAHAM: Sir?

HARRISON: I've come from Dr Halley. He says you must see me.

GRAHAM: *Must*, sir?

HARRISON: Talk with me, sir.

GRAHAM: *Must*, sir?

HARRISON: Recommend.

GRAHAM: *Must*, sir?

HARRISON: If you please, sir.

GRAHAM: Please. Good. I like people to say 'please'.

HARRISON: I'm not much spun on niceties, sir.

GRAHAM: Niceties are what keep us off each other's throats, Mr– ?

HARRISON: Harrison. John Harrison. I've no design on throats, neither.

GRAHAM: I'm glad to hear it. Your business?

HARRISON: I have ideas for a clock at sea.

GRAHAM: We all have.

HARRISON: One that'll work accurately.

GRAHAM: One you *think* will work accurately.

HARRISON: One I *know* will work accurately.

GRAHAM: I've not much time for people who know things they can't know.

HARRISON: I can't help knowing what I know and I know my sea clock will work as my land clock does.

GRAHAM: You've built an *accurate* land clock?

HARRISON: Loses one second in a month.

GRAHAM: A boast indeed.

HARRISON: I boast not nor play not. I know what I know, I make what I make, and what I make I know the worth of, and I have in my house one pendulum clock that has not varied as much as a whole minute in ten years.

GRAHAM: Oil. The problem of expanding oil – how did you stop it expanding?

HARRISON: I didn't. Just stopped using metal on metal which needed the oil.

> GRAHAM *is impressed. Attentive now. Even excited*

GRAHAM: How can a clock run without metal wheels?

HARRISON: By using wooden ones instead.

GRAHAM: Wooden wheels?

HARRISON: I'm a carpenter. I know the properties of wood. Pivots of brass move easily in hard wood. No oil.

GRAHAM: And pendulums? I've never made a pendulum that kept the rhythm of its swing because the damn things kept expanding and contracting in different weathers.

HARRISON: But not all metals expand and contract to the same degree.

GRAHAM: So?

HARRISON: So. . . [*unwrapping gridiron from cloth*] . . . if you place brass alongside steel expanding and contracting at different rates you produce a gridiron that compensates for the expansion of the pendulum.

GRAHAM: And on sea? How can you make pendulums swing evenly in high seas?

HARRISON: Don't use pendulums.

GRAHAM: What moves the seconds on if not a pendulum?

HARRISON: Springs!

GRAHAM: Springs?

HARRISON: Springs, sir. Springs dingaling.

GRAHAM: What kind of springs?

HARRISON: Spiral springs.
GRAHAM: And you've structured such springs?
HARRISON: I'm working on them.
GRAHAM: Springs? Nothing else?
HARRISON: Springs and things.
GRAHAM: What things?
HARRISON: Well – bars and balances that swing on the springs.
GRAHAM: Drawings, have you got drawings?
HARRISON: It so happens –

Withdraws rolls of paper from knapsack.

GRAHAM: Oh, my word.
HARRISON: But I need help.
GRAHAM: Oh, my word, my word, my word.

GRAHAM *is riveted by the drawings.*

HARRISON: Help?
GRAHAM: I'll make you a loan.

Elizabeth's Kitchen

ELIZABETH: That's how it all began –
GRAHAM: £500.
ELIZABETH: – sweetly and kindly.
GRAHAM: Pay me back when you can. No interest. And I'll talk to others. We'll get you started, Mr Harrison, so's you can find us longitude and save lives.
ELIZABETH: [*The Litany*] Too late to save the *Vansittart*, ninety-six lives lost, silver bullion, copper, lead, or the *King George*, fifty-four lives lost, iron, wool, cloth . . .

The streets come alive.

Bustle. Music. Street cries.

Harrison's Workshop

HARRISON *and* ELIZABETH.

ELIZABETH: [*to* HARRISON] What does it mean – 'find us longitude'? Is it something us once had and lost? Is it something we know is out there and needs to be found? And why is it so difficult to find it?

> HARRISON *wheels on globe of the world.*

> [*NOTE: what follows could perhaps be a kind of light show demonstrating why it is easier to identify latitude than longitude. Spectacular. Magical.*]

HARRISON: The world is round.
ELIZABETH: You didn't marry an ignorant woman, John Harrison.
HARRISON: But I married an argumentative one.
ELIZABETH: Pot calling the kettle black, is it?
HARRISON: And one who must have the last word.
ELIZABETH: Your globe, your globe!
HARRISON: Me globe! Me globe! The round earth – right?

> *Pause.*

Imagine. The sea. Vast. Empty. A ship, its captain, its crew, its cargo. A mist descends. Where are they? Are they north or south, east or west?

> *Pause.*

To find out where we are on this globe the mapmakers devised imaginary lines that go round the earth which they called latitudes;

and imaginary lines that go from pole to pole which they called longitudes.

Now, Lizzie, my love, it's easy for the captain to fix his latitude, to find out how far north or south he is because nature helps him. The sun. He's got the sun, which identifies the equator. The sun dictates, the circles are drawn, the captain knows where he is north or south. He knows. Easy!

But what about east and west? What dictates the other imaginary lines, the longitudes?

ELIZABETH *spreads her arms, shrugs.*

Spin the globe.

She spins it.

And follow this: the earth takes twenty-four hours to spin three hundred and sixty degrees from sun back to sun – a day. It takes twenty-four hours for us, here where we live, to move from one high noon to the next. So, how far have we moved in an hour?

Pause.

There they are: three hundred and sixty degrees – twenty-four hours.

Pause.

Divide one into the other – twenty-four into three hundred and sixty, and you get fifteen. In one hour we've moved fifteen degrees east or west.

Pause.

Am I losing you, Lizzie?

ELIZABETH: You will if you keep stopping to see if I'm breathing. In one hour we've moved fifteen degrees east or west.

HARRISON: But how does the poor captain know? There's no equator for longitude like there is for latitude. No sun to help. So what *can* help?

Long pause.

Clocks! To chart his longitude at sea a captain needs to know, at the very same moment, the time on board and the time he left port. The difference is the distance he's travelled.

He watches her carefully.

You don't follow?

She shakes her head.

If he had two clocks the captain would reset the ship's clock by the sun, compare it to the home port's clock, and every hour of difference would tell him he'd moved fifteen degrees east or west.

Waits and watches.

ELIZABETH: But, John my love, you said there are no clocks can work at sea.

HARRISON: Yet! No captain can tell if he's travelled fifteen degrees or thirty degrees. Yet!

And if he's sailing in fog no captain knows if he's sailing into rocks or reefs or sandbanks or pirates or friendly harbours or death. Yet!

But John Harrison will tell them, he'll make them the clock they need. Yes, he will, yes. Oh will he not! Yes, yes, John Harrison will he will.

ELIZABETH: And John Harrison did he did. He made them their clock.

As HARRISON *wheels off his globe the first clock – Clock One – is lit up in his workshop.*

The streets come alive.

Bustle. Music. Street cries.

Harrison's Workshop

HALLEY *and* GRAHAM *walking round and round Clock One.*

ELIZABETH: Anyway, four years after George Graham's generosity, he ups to London with Clock One. A monster. Beautiful but huge. Nothing like it had been seen before.

HALLEY: He'll get the London chinwags wagging their chins over this.

GRAHAM: When I made my clocks I was in touch with the best craftsmen of the day. *You've* worked it all out for yourself, Harrison.

HARRISON: Thank you. Yes.

HALLEY: We've got to get this before the Longitude Board.

HARRISON: Thank you. Yes. I should be most grateful.

GRAHAM: The Longitude Board? Aren't they all dead?

HALLEY: Ignore him, Harrison. He's famous for jesting.

GRAHAM: We could exhume them.

HALLEY: Be serious, George.

GRAHAM: I've given the man money to complete his lovely thing. What could be more serious, eh, Harrison?

HARRISON: I shall always be grateful.

GRAHAM: Even though bemused.

HARRISON: Confused, I think. I've never understood the point of jesting.

HALLEY: We'll show this to the Royal Society. The Board will *have* to take notice if *they* recommend, too. And we'll get the Admiralty to give the beast a practical test aboard one of its ships.

GRAHAM: I don't know why you're getting excited about all this, Halley. You're a lunar man. Never trust a lunar man, Harrison, he thinks he's in touch with God.

They leave.

HARRISON *returns to help* ELIZABETH *pull and stretch washed sheets.*

A Tavern

HALLEY *and* GRAHAM.

FOLKES, *President of the Royal Society, approaches.*

FOLKES: The Royal Society has little interest in mechanical solutions to longitude. If one of the brightest minds in the land were enamoured of it we might show more enthusiasm.

HALLEY: I *am* one of the brightest minds in the land, Folkes.

FOLKES: And you're a lunar man, Halley.

HALLEY: I'm also a scientist, and that means keeping an open mind.

FOLKES: I'm not denying Harrison is clever. Clever, he's clever. Can't deny that. But a carpenter! From Lincolnshire! Really! No background, no education. Who'll take him seriously? And consider it – a mechanical timekeeper competing with God's heavens. Why else give us stars if not to guide us by?

GRAHAM: To count, perhaps? Get to sleep more easily?

FOLKES: And Halley's mapped the heavens.

HALLEY: And been at it a long time, too, Folkes, imagining that longitude would be known only by the intricate motion of the moon. But in the end I could see – her motions are *too* intricate, the results could only be attended with great error.

FOLKES: How can that be? Sailors have means to measure distances between sun, moon and stars.

HALLEY: But not precisely. Your study of astronomy has taught you nothing if you can't see the lunar lady is erratic and unpredictable. She defies precise measurement. She can't be pinned down.

FOLKES: But she has been! The lunar lady's subtle ways are becoming known.

HALLEY: The lunar lady's tables were calculated on land, the sailors have to make adjustments for sea levels. Their sheets become unreadable, full of rectifying calculations.

FOLKES: And doesn't all that difficulty suggest that the lunar method must be right?

Incredulous silence.

Harrison's Workshop

HARRISON: And then – along comes a ticking thing in a box invented not by a priest or professor but by an uneducated carpenter. A ticking thing in a box! Ha! A clock! Oh my goodness deary me. Tick tock tick tock! A clock! Oh deary deary me. Tick tock tick tock!

Long, reflective pause.

Do I have regrets? Were there words wrong I uttered? If I'm ill-used is the fault mine? It's beholden upon me to ask – are there other ways I could have behaved?

Pause.

I've proposed laws for music and argued that a note pitched even the tiniest degree off those laws will sound ill, not truly sweet. And I must wonder – is there in life a tone of speaking that is also not truly sweet if not pitched according to the same laws? Perhaps I didn't tune myself sweetly enough to be listened to. Perhaps, though time has *obsessed* me, I'm *out* of time. I've made clocks accurate for land and sea but perhaps nothing tick tocks accurately in me. I must ask these things.

Considers such possibilities.

But not for long.

Nay! Nay nay nay! I began sweetly and honestly and trustingly enough until they abused my trust. They spout nonsense whereas my clocks, I make bold to say, my timekeepers for longitude are the most beautiful and curious mechanical thing in the world, and I heartily thank Almighty God that I have lived so long as in some measure to complete it. So –

Burst of choral music.

Sing out you weavers! Sing out you smithies! Sing out you shoemakers, printers, carpenters and boys. Sing out!

The streets come alive.

Bustle. Music. Street cries.

Clanging bell.

Announcement Platform

COMMISSIONER: [*reading*] 'John Harrison's machine for measuring time at sea, having been constructed with great labour and expense, seems to the members of the Royal Society to promise sufficient exactness as to deserve public encouragement to be tried and improved.'

Red Lion Square

ELIZABETH: And so, Clock One was given a trial on board a ship. Not to the West Indies which the Act of Queen Anne called for, but to Lisbon. Took a week to get there and four weeks to get back and my poor John was sick as a dog. But on the journey back – listen to this –

Cries of 'land ahoy'.

Heaving Ship's Cabin

A sick HARRISON *holding fast to Clock One.*

Master of the ship, ROGER WILLS, *looking down on a map.*

WILLS: Well, according to my reckoning the land ahoy is the Start Point.

HARRISON: That was a dead-reckoning, with respect, Master Wills.

WILLS: Good God, man, 'tis you I reckon looks dead.

HARRISON: My legs were made for dry land. The sea is for fish.

WILLS: Don't let my men hear you say that. Here –

Offers him a bottle.

– good rum.

HARRISON *retches.*

Not here, man, for God's sake not here!

HARRISON *recovers.*

HARRISON: Dropping flotsam in the water and counting as you go past it to measure speed and plot course belongs to the days of Columbus.

WILLS: So you're about to tell me land ahoy is not Start Point.

HARRISON: No, Master Wills, with respect, Master Wills –

He retches again.

WILLS: Not here! Not here!

HARRISON *recovers again.*

HARRISON: According to my clock, and according to my observations, the land ahoy is the spot known as Lizard.

Red Lion Square

ELIZABETH: And he was right, and the Master writes him out a certificate of proof. Well, you'd think after that the man would want his clock tested on the West Indies run to win the £20,000 prize. Not my John.

HARRISON: I'm not satisfied, Lizzie. I can do better. The beast is unwieldy. Got to make it smaller. More manageable. I won't have Clock One tested again. I won't!

ELIZABETH: And when he won't he won't! Instead, he asks the Board for £500 to work on a second clock. They agree. But on conditions. £250 now, and £250 when he completes the second clock after which, now listen to this, after which he's got to hand over *both* to the nation.

HARRISON: Which is not right, I know, Lizzie love, not just. They had no hand in the making of Clock One and no right to claim it. But we need to live, don't we? And I need peace of mind to go on to the next stage.

ELIZABETH: And so you'd better agree, my love.

HARRISON: I will, Lizzie, I will.

ELIZABETH: And I give birth to William. Don't ask me why but we all seemed to name our children William or John, Anne or Jane, or Elizabeth. John and me we had William and Elizabeth. My Elizabeth married a John and gave birth to a John. William married an Elizabeth and gave birth to a John who married a Jane and gave birth to a John. His third wife was also an Elizabeth who gave birth to an Anne who married a John and gave birth to an Elizabeth. See how time flies?

	Clocks One and Two make John famous if not rich.
HARRISON:	Professor Halley dies.
ELIZABETH:	The Board of Longitude give John another £500 to work on Clock Three; the first is in George Graham's shop window; we move to this big house here in Red Lion Square –
HARRISON:	And William Hogarth draws Clock One in a print and says: 'One of the most exquisite movements ever made,' he says.
ELIZABETH:	And John Harrison Esquire gets awarded the Copley Gold Medal.

Clanging bell.

Announcement Platform

The award ceremony. FOLKES *delivering award speech.*

FOLKES: And so we, honourable members of the Royal Society of which I, Martin Folkes, am proud to be President, are in no doubt therefore why the Copley Gold Medal is so deserved. A restless genius! Lived near a seaport! Heard of the importance of longitude, and became inquisitive, as genius does. What if he could construct a clock to endure the violent and irregular motions of a boisterous sea?

Amazingly he knew: two major changes must be made. Springs must replace weights, and regular motion must come from the vibrations of balances and not the swinging of pendulums. The problems were enormous. Metal plates, screws, springs, brass weights, steel rods, wheels, cylinders – dozens of strange new parts and contrivances all had to be drawn, described, machined, tested, machined again, tested again, re-thought, re-drawn, machined again, tested again. What painstaking attention to detail. It confounds imagination.

And soon he hopes to test Clock Three on a voyage to the West Indies, as the Act requires. And although John Harrison is one of the most modest men I know yet he assures me, without doubt, that having put his timepiece through the most accurate experiments it will keep time constantly without the variation of so much as three seconds in a week. Astonishing! Stupendous!

ELIZABETH: Well, I don't know about 'the most modest of men'.

Harrison's Workshop

By the time John is sixty-four the bulk of the work is done on the third clock. He's ready to let it be tested.

But before it was finished something else was afoot. John, mindful of the cramped quarters in a captain's cabin, was aiming at compactness. Clock Three was about as small as he could get it – two feet high one foot wide. That is until –

> HARRISON *is dangling a pocket watch, opens it, looks at the interior through a magnifying glass. Something is dawning on him.*

HARRISON: It's small. Light. Could be, could be. Ha! Ha! Ho! Ho! Could be, could be. Let them get stiff necks gazing up at stars, let them go mad chasing the moon, let them go blind in one eye from measuring distance from the sun – but down here, feet on the ground, in the palm of my hand here could be the answer. Not a clock but a watch!

Admiralty

Meeting of the Board of Longitude.

LORDS EGMONT *and* MORTON, *and* REV. MASKELYNE *in attendance listening to* HARRISON.

HARRISON: I'm aware, good sirs, of your patience, your indulgence and your encouraging generosity, and my third timekeeper is nigh on complete.
MORTON: Twenty years in the making, Harrison.
HARRISON: In the making, Lord Morton, *and* the designing *and* the testing *and* the redesigning *and* the making of a living meanwhile.
EGMONT: We can expect it when?
HARRISON: Soon, Lord Egmont, soon. But this time, my Lords and – er – Reverend Maskelyne, I bring other news.
MORTON: This meeting must end soon, Harrison. We live busy lives.
HARRISON: We all live busy lives, sir, and so for my own sake I won't keep you much longer. It's this.

He produces the pocket watch.

Recently made for me to my own design and specifications, and for my personal use.

ACT ONE

> Beats true come hot or cold, and it doesn't stop dead when you wind it up.
>
> *Dangles it high.*
>
> Small. Compact. Not even *I* thought it possible, but now I have good reason to think that this small thing – not my huge beasts – this lovely handful could be the forerunner of such small machines as maybe of great service with respect to the longitude.

EGMONT: And you have it in mind to make such?

HARRISON: More than have it in mind, sir. My drawings are begun. I'm racing ahead.

EGMONT: What do you say to that, Maskelyne? [*to* HARRISON] Maskelyne here is on the verge of proving the lunar method as the only sound method of finding longitude.

HARRISON: I've heard it.

MORTON: And could it be, Mr Harrison, that having heard it you're racing ahead for fear the lunar method will prove your tick-tocking clock redundant? Could it be you *fear* heaven's clock?

> HARRISON's *response stiffens the air with his contempt.*

HARRISON: Heaven has no clock! The stars are for *God* to find his way around, not men. The maker of all things made mists and storms for the confusion of mankind, and to mankind he gave the power to invent a way out of the confusion.

MORTON: Battle lines drawn, I think.

> *The streets come alive.*
>
> *Bustle. Music. Street cries.*

Red Lion Square

ELIZABETH *in her kitchen.*

HARRISON *and son,* WILLIAM, *in workshop.*

ELIZABETH: And the lines *were* drawn for battle. Battles to break the heart of the strongest. Did you notice one man who said nothing, him that was born same year as my daughter, Elizabeth, God rest her? Rev. Nevil Maskelyne.

HARRISON: Him with three chins and no hair.

WILLIAM: Hush now, father.

ELIZABETH: You tell him, son.

WILLIAM: *You* tell him, mother. Wives have moral authority, sons are slaves or upstarts.

HARRISON: Is that what you think I think of you?

WILLIAM: I jest, father. I jest.

HARRISON: Why does everyone jest? Because I don't want thee at my side reluctantly.

WILLIAM: It's city life. Can't be caught being too solemn.

HARRISON: As long as tha's not caught talking nonsense like him.

ELIZABETH: Like who?

WILLIAM & HARRISON: [*together*] Him with three chins and no hair.

Admiralty/Red Lion Square

Meeting of the Board of Longitude: MASKELYNE, MORTON *and* EGMONT.

HARRISON *barracks with 'asides' to the amusement of his son and wife.*

MASKELYNE: The lunar method for finding longitude is both simple and complicated.

HARRISON: Both at once! The man lives in a fog.
MASKELYNE: Simple because it merely requires looking at the moon –
HARRISON: If the night sky is not covered with clouds, that is.
MASKELYNE: – which moves in relationship to the stars which are fixed.
HARRISON: And can only be seen if the night sky isn't covered by clouds, that is.
MASKELYNE: And it's complicated because the path of the moon is so erratic –
HARRISON: And often covered by clouds, that is.
MASKELYNE: – so that it was considered impossible to record and tabulate its position.
HARRISON: Because the bloody thing was covered by clouds, that is.
MASKELYNE: However, in recent years lunar tables have been produced which will enable our navigators to find longitude with the sextant which is replacing the quadrant –
HARRISON: – and doesn't make a ha'p'orth of difference because our navigators can't see through the bloody clouds.

Great laughter from WILLIAM *and* ELIZABETH *over which the* CHOIR *breaks into choral song.*

That's right, my lads. Drown his nonsense with singing. Harmony over chaos!
ELIZABETH: [*over the singing*] And now Clock Three is ready to be tested at sea. John is too old to make the journey. And so – who else but his son, our son, William, loyal, devoted, hardworking.
WILLIAM: Though I'd sooner live the life of a city gentleman than a defender of clocks. But who

can resist such a father who I admire for his brilliance, love for his kindness, and resent for chaining my life to his marvellous obsession – a timepiece!

ELIZABETH: The Board gave William £250 to kit himself out, sent him to Portsmouth to await further instructions, and left him there for five months!

WILLIAM: Five months! In Portsmouth!

HARRISON: Oh, worthy powers that be! Oh, worthy authority! Oh, eminent men of science who can make or break.

WILLIAM: Making me wait! Playing for time while Maskelyne checks his lunar tables and men die.

Sounds of shipwreck at sea:

Timber shattering on rock.

Human voices in distress.

Elizabeth's Kitchen

She is laying a table. As she does so she chants.

ELIZABETH: [*The Litany*] The *Sussex*, ten lives, tea, silk, chinaware, lacquer ware. The *Grantham*, ninety-six lives, cotton, a hundred tons of pepper, twenty tons of cloves, mace, nutmeg . . .

The crying dies away.

HARRISON *and* WILLIAM *take their place round the table.*

It's always the kitchen. We have a lovely dining room but we always gather in the kitchen.

WILLIAM:	All families do, mother.
ELIZABETH:	And get in your way.
WILLIAM:	But you love it.
ELIZABETH:	Chatter when you're cooking –
WILLIAM:	– pick at food with their fingers –
ELIZABETH:	– complain that it's lamb when it's pork, and pork when it's lamb.
WILLIAM:	You wouldn't have it any other way.
ELIZABETH:	Oh, I wouldn't, wouldn't I?
WILLIAM:	And I'll miss you when you're gone!

Kisses her.

ELIZABETH:	I think *I'll* miss me when I'm gone, too! [*Beat.*] What's wrong with your father?
WILLIAM:	Father, what's wrong with you?
HARRISON:	Nothing's wrong. I'm thinking.
WILLIAM:	He's thinking.
ELIZABETH:	No he's not. I know when he's thinking – he looks up at the ceiling.
WILLIAM:	Well he's looking down now.
ELIZABETH:	Which means he's decided.
HARRISON:	Not the clock!
ELIZABETH:	What 'not the clock'?
HARRISON:	I'm not sending Clock Three for the West Indies trial.
ELIZABETH:	You must send the clock for trial.
WILLIAM:	We've told the Board we would.
HARRISON:	The watch must go instead.
WILLIAM:	The watch?
HARRISON:	We must offer the watch for trial.
WILLIAM:	But it's not ready, father.
HARRISON:	It'll be ready.
WILLIAM:	If we fail this trial we fail for all time.
HARRISON:	The watch won't fail.
WILLIAM:	All your years wasted.

HARRISON: I am not letting those priests and professors take a foothold with their daft lunar theories. They're only happy in the clouds, stargazing to no avail, thinking they're in communion with God. I'll not let them deprive me of a fair trial.

ELIZABETH: I'm glad we're all together – father, mother and son –

A warm, domestic moment.

WILLIAM: Even though we're in the kitchen!

ELIZABETH: Especially because you're in the kitchen.

HARRISON: [*leaving*] Right! You've got your kitchen, I've got me workshop.

ELIZABETH: No, don't go, for I want something explained. There's some of it I understand and some of it I don't understand; and some of it I don't care to understand and some of it I *want* to understand.

HARRISON: Get on with it, woman.

ELIZABETH: Don't you be impatient with me, John Harrison, save that for –

HARRISON: – for me priests and professors. I will, Lizzie, I will.

ELIZABETH: Two things. First – what's 'the rate'?

WILLIAM: 'The rate' is what we tell the Board of Longitude we think the watch will lose by each day.

They wait for a sign that she's understood.

ELIZABETH: Ah!

Pause.

Why?

WILLIAM: Because if our watch loses the same amount each day and not wildly differing amounts each day then it can be depended upon to help us find longitude.

They wait for a sign that she's understood.

ELIZABETH: You mean if it loses half a second one day and fourteen seconds the next day you'll be all at sea?
HARRISON: Correct.

Long pause.

ELIZABETH: Next: How do you know what rate to tell them?
WILLIAM: That's why father has been locked away in his workshop – testing and adjusting.
ELIZABETH: Testing and adjusting. Ah!
WILLIAM: Fine tuning.
ELIZABETH: Fine tuning. Ah!

HARRISON *sweeps up his wife in a kind of jig, singing –*

HARRISON: Ah! Ah! Tick a leary
Tick tock tick my deary.
Ah! Ah! Tick a leary
Tick tock tick my deary.

Over which come the sounds of wind and waves. Not a storm, just a ship at sea.

Clanging bell.

Announcement Platform

COMMISSIONER: [*reading*] 'The plans for the trial of the Harrison watch at sea in H.M.S. *Deptford* are clear-cut. One: The box containing the watch to be fitted with four different locks.

Two: The keys to be retained by travellers on the boat. Three: Mr Robertson – Master of the Portsmouth Royal Academy – will calculate local time and record corresponding time of the watch in the presence of Captain Hughes, Captain Digges, and William Harrison. Four: Prior to sailing, Mr Robertson in the presence of same witnesses to set watch to local time. Five: Mr Robertson, on landing in Jamaica, will ascertain local time there and compare it with time of watch – all to be witnessed and the results sealed and forwarded to the Admiralty.'

> *Sound of wind and sea rise to storm level, beginning halfway through previous speech and finally taking over.*

Ship's Cabin

> WILLIAM, *wrapped and struggling to stand in a cabin heaving and wet, enacting what he's describing.*

WILLIAM: That was a voyage I feared would end my days. The return was hell. A sea of monsters with gaping jaws, and a great marvel to me that our timepiece kept going at all. I placed it in the captain's cabin. Driest place, he said. But when the sea struck, the water flowed in through every joint. Sometimes two feet of water on deck and five inches deep in the cabin. Six weeks and never a dry inch. How did I keep the watch box dry in all that you're wondering? Kept it wrapped in a blanket; and when that became soaked I squeezed it out and covered it with another and another and another. And when I ran out of dry blankets I slept in one so that my body heat dried it some, which led to me being racked with a fever. Add that to seasickness, and I was left ill as I never hope to be again. But – the watch ticked on. Amazing! And lost only one minute fifty-four and a half seconds in a hundred and forty-seven days. One minute fifty-four and a half seconds in a hundred and forty-seven days! The £20,000 prize was ours! A watch to find longitude the world over! Who could dispute it?

Storm dies away.

ELIZABETH: The Board of Longitude, that's who.
HARRISON: Priests and professors!
ELIZABETH: They met and called William to account. The procedures laid down had not, they said, been followed.

Admiralty

WILLIAM, EGMONT *and* MORTON.

EGMONT: Our most urgent objection is to do with the rate of loss. The return journey from Jamaica in the *Merlin* was not conducted under supervision. Without supervision we cannot eliminate the possibility of tampering.
WILLIAM: The Act doesn't say the return journey is part of the official test.
MORTON: No matter. You're claiming the watch lost one minute fifty-four and a half seconds in

	a hundred and forty-seven days there and back.
WILLIAM:	Forget the return journey. Look to the journey just from Portsmouth to Jamaica. In eighty-one days our timekeeper lost only 5.1 seconds.
MORTON:	Yes, if you take into account an *agreed* daily rate of loss.
WILLIAM:	We *have* taken into account a daily rate of loss – 2.66 seconds a day.
MORTON:	A loss that was not agreed upon in advance.
HARRISON:	Priests and professors!
WILLIAM:	It wasn't *asked* for in advance.

The streets come alive.

HARRISON: Priests and professors! They keep moving the damn target.

Bustle. Music. Street cries.

Red Lion Square

WILLIAM, HARRISON *and* ELIZABETH.

WILLIAM:	It seems like this, father. The Board is not seriously questioning my procedure with anything but the calculating of the rate. They say we should have declared that rate before leaving.
HARRISON:	Maskelyne. Him. The Reverend bastard Maskelyne.
WILLIAM:	He's not on the Board, father. Forget the man.
HARRISON:	Not *on* the Board maybe but he knows the Board. Every one of them. They know each other.

ELIZABETH: Forget the man.
HARRISON: Priests and professors!
ELIZABETH: You'll drive yourself mad.
HARRISON: Talk among themselves.
ELIZABETH: Forget them.
HARRISON: Tittle tattle tittle tattle!
WILLIAM: Father! I'm none too certain myself.

Pause.

HARRISON: Thee! Not certain!
WILLIAM: We *should* have declared the rate of loss beforehand, and I'm not sure that the rate of loss we decided on *after* the voyage was any but rough and ready.
HARRISON: So what do us do now?
WILLIAM: The commissioners have decided that to clear up the doubts and differences of opinion there should be another trial run to the West Indies.
ELIZABETH: Another?
HARRISON: I'll agree to that.
ELIZABETH: Risk his life and your timekeeper?
HARRISON: If it will end all disputes, I'll agree.
ELIZABETH: Your son's life and your life's work?
WILLIAM: But that's not all, father.

Admiralty/Harrison's Workshop

EGMONT, MORTON, WILLIAM *and* HARRISON.

EGMONT: Our problem is, we need it explained *before* it goes back to sea for a second trial run. We don't really understand what makes it run so regularly.
MORTON: After all, what if you and the watch sank in a disaster?

EGMONT: What we want, Mr Harrison, are examples of the tools you used –

HARRISON: Oh, yes?

EGMONT: – so that craftsmen can reproduce them for making copies of the watch.

HARRISON: Oh, yes, yes?

EGMONT: Then we want you to dismantle the watch piece by piece –

HARRISON: Yes, yes.

EGMONT: – and explain what each piece does.

HARRISON: Oh? Really?

EGMONT: We will further require you to supervise the making of two more watches.

HARRISON: Just two? Not four? Not six? Not ten?

EGMONT: And finally we will need to test those watches to see if, when made by other workmen, they'll work with equal efficiency.

HARRISON: And who will protect my rights when all is known?

EGMONT: Your rights will be protected. We are proposing new legislation.

HARRISON: Will you advance me £5000 in support of your promise to protect my rights?

MORTON: *Not* five thousand! Fifteen hundred now and a further one thousand after the second sea trial.

EGMONT: All of this will be written into the new legislation.

HARRISON: I'm seventy for heaven's sake. What good is money to me in my grave? Mean little minds you have. You make me ashamed to be English and I'll say no no no no as long as I have a drop of English blood in my body.

EGMONT: Sir, I have not heard talk like that before, never!

HARRISON: Then, sir, it's about time you did hear talk like that, for if this goes on, you, your professors and your priests will find reasons and more reasons for not awarding me my due, or you'll prevaricate and find tasks and seek guarantees and safeguards – none of which is required in the first Act of Queen Anne of fifty years ago.

EGMONT: Sir, you –

HARRISON: And ships will wreck themselves upon rocks and women and children made widows and orphans.

EGMONT: Mr Harrison, you are the strangest and most obstinate creature –

HARRISON: Me? Obstinate? Have none of you any idea how long it will take to prepare written descriptions and working drawings of the mechanisms and then, *then* make two watches?

EGMONT: Mr Harrison, sir –

HARRISON: Sir sir sir!

EGMONT: – if you would but do what we want you to do, and which is in your power to do, I will give you my word to give you the money if you will but do it.

HARRISON: And I know too well *why* you want me to do it. Yes, sir, I do, sir. Indeed I do, sir.

MORTON: Why, tell us, sir, what evil, underhand connivances do you suppose this illustrious body of men are up to? Eh? What dastardly schemes, pray, are you imputing?

HARRISON: That while my timekeeper is dismantled and out of function your priest and professor the very very oh so reverend Nevil Maskelyne will seek a trial of the lunar-tic method with its mad and cumbersome measurements between fixed stars and a crazy moon. And you'll love that, all of you. Your little heads will look up and gaze at the magnificence of the heavens and you'll imagine God is speaking to you, telling you the way, and it won't matter if there's a cloud or two or three or four you'll wait till they're passed and waste time calculating when all you need is my little piece of machinery. But no! Oh no! Too vulgar for you. What's a little metal, a few springs, and tiny wheels compared to the stars? Good Lord and little fishes! Who is this upstart from up north with his tick tocking cogs and balances?

Well I'll tell you who I am. I'm John Harrison from Barrow-on-Humber, and I'm seventy years old, and I've given half my life to solving the one problem could make this country the greatest maritime nation in the world, and you little men with your tawdry conditions for this to be done first and that to be done first and everything to be done first before I receive my just rewards, you little men of theory – you're squeezing the blood out of my last years. Oh, yes. I know only too well why you want my timekeeper dismantled.

MORTON: And we know only too well why dismantle it you will not.
HARRISON: Which is?
MORTON: You fear your timekeeper is not ready.
HARRISON: Let the second sea trial be judge of that, shall we, Lord Morton?
EGMONT: And let us hope all will proceed simply from here on.

Barbados/Harrison's Workshop/ Elizabeth's Kitchen

A temporary observatory is being erected on the sands in Barbados by MASKELYNE *and his assistant.*

HARRISON *and* WILLIAM *are in their workshop.* ELIZABETH *in her kitchen.*

ELIZABETH: And did it proceed simply? Nothing to do with my John could ever be simple. Up came pen and paper again – he reached for his quill as some reach for their sword – and off he wrote at once to the Board of Longitude requesting that new conditions for the second trial at sea be clearly stated.

Finally, after much unpleasant argument, William boarded the H.M.S. *Tartar*, and set sail for Barbados again. And then came the big row. When William arrived in Barbados who did he find but the Reverend Maskelyne, who'd been sent ahead in order to determine the exact moment of noon, and compare it to the hour on our timekeeper. But on the way to their makeshift observatory, now listen to this, William heard someone saying, 'Here comes the other competitor for the prize!' The *'other'* competitor for the prize?

Observatory in Barbados

MASKELYNE *and* WILLIAM.

MASKELYNE: No matter what you heard, sir, there was nothing of ill intent on my part.

WILLIAM: No ill intent? Who talked to people here about his work on the lunar theory and his hope that it would gain the prize?

MASKELYNE: And if so?

WILLIAM: And if so then how could you be impartial in providing calculations on our behalf since they might favour an alternative to your lunar theory?

MASKELYNE: You should have made known your qualms to the Board before I left.

WILLIAM: We did.

MASKELYNE: And were assured of my integrity.

WILLIAM: And assured, too, that your instructions were to do everything to ensure the proper execution of this test.

MASKELYNE: Which I have done, am doing, and will continue to do.

WILLIAM: Then what business was it of yours to lord your lunar theories all over the place?

MASKELYNE: Please, Mr Harrison, lower your voice, do. In six months here is it to be imagined I would not talk of work that has occupied me all these years? There had never been any secret about my interest and support of the lunar method. In fact the Board themselves instructed me to test the accuracy of the new lunar tables, which I have done, and was able to predict the longitude of Barbados to within half a degree. Would you deny me sharing my enthusiasms? Was I to remain silent about my own experiments because the Harrison timekeeper was on its way? I have been a man of science since my youth and what matters to me are my integrity and scientific truth. You have no reason to doubt either, sir. And I bid you good day.

Red Lion Square

ELIZABETH, HARRISON *and* WILLIAM.

ELIZABETH: Well, they didn't exactly kiss and make up. Their quarrels died away as quarrels do. Maskelyne took his readings, thoroughly checked the timekeeper, and everything was sent back to the Admiralty for the next stage. And do you hear how I can now talk with ease about scientific matters?

When the Board met in January my men were not invited. Four mathematicians were called instead, and each declared that the watch had accuracy three times better than was required to win the full £20,000. Success! A lifetime of endeavour was about to be crowned with fame and fortune. But was it?

HARRISON: No! Was the fortune placed in my bank? No! Was the crown of fame placed on my head? No! Was glory and honour bestowed? No, no, no! Now why? Ask me why?

ELIZABETH: They found out when the Board eventually summoned them.

Admiralty

EGMONT, MORTON, MASKELYNE, WILLIAM *and* HARRISON.

MORTON: May I remind the Board that a section of the Act of King George has yet to be satisfied?

HARRISON: Oh? And which one is that, my ever so lordly Lord Morton?

MORTON: You lack respect, sir. Your nature is intemperate.

HARRISON: My nature is blunt.
MORTON: Blunt natures do not by nature command the truth.
HARRISON: What has my nature to do with the truth? Truth resides in facts. The facts are simple. There was a problem – longitude. There was a prize for solving the problem – I solved the problem. The prize is in all honour mine.
EGMONT: If only the world were that black and white, Mr Harrison.
HARRISON: It is, my Lord Egmont. Black and white. Good and evil. Right and wrong. If you see it muddy it's because your priests and professors muddy clear waters.
EGMONT: It is not that clear waters are muddied, but that human motivation renders the human condition grey. Grey, Mr Harrison, grey. Which means nothing is simple.
HARRISON: The results of the mathematicians' calculations were favourable to the watch. Simple! I wrote to the Board requesting humbly ever so humbly that they grant me the authority to claim the prize. Simple!
EGMONT: Not simple. We couldn't grant you that authority because not all the Board members were present at that meeting. One man in particular had to be party to any such decision.
HARRISON: And that man was?
EGMONT: While the Barbados trial was taking place Dr Bliss, the Astronomer Royal, died, and it was my pleasure to inform the Board that the King had approved the appointment of the Reverend Nevil Maskelyne.
HARRISON: Another reverend in command!

ACT ONE

MASKELYNE: You misjudge me, Mr Harrison, as your son misjudged me, as indeed you misjudge everyone and all things. I've called this Board meeting just twenty-one days after my appointment because I consider the issue of great importance.

HARRISON: Aye! To the nation, sir.

MASKELYNE: Of course to the nation, sir.

HARRISON: The poor damned sailors of His Majesty's navy who have to sail blindfold while you fart around my invention which anyone can see –

WILLIAM: Father, be quiet. This is a time for reason not anger.

HARRISON: Then you be reasonable with them. I give you my blessing.

MASKELYNE: We are all agreed that your timekeeper kept its time with sufficient correctness on the voyage from Portsmouth to Barbados.

WILLIAM: It did better than that.

MASKELYNE: Yes, the minutes will record it did better than that.

WILLIAM: It kept time with correctness beyond the limits laid down by the Act of Queen Anne.

MASKELYNE: Even *considerably* beyond the limits laid down by the Act of Queen Anne.

HARRISON: But? But? Don't we hear a 'but' in your tone of voice?

EGMONT: Quiet, Mr Harrison. It's time for quiet now.

MORTON: Yes he does hear a 'but' – let's stop pussyfooting around the man. The section of the Act of King George that I wanted to remind the Board is still operative is the one that calls for the invention to be practical, practical and useful at sea, and the only way we

	can ascertain this is for you to dismantle your watch as you agreed in '63 and prove it is a mechanism easy to replicate.
EGMONT:	Replicate! Replicate! As you agreed.
HARRISON:	I agreed on conditions.
MASKELYNE:	And those conditions were accepted and written into the new Act of King George – your invention to be protected, and no other person allowed to claim a reward for a timekeeper until judgement had been passed on the merits of your watch.
MORTON:	And the time has come to judge its merits. It is not enough that your timekeeper found longitude, it must also be capable of easy manufacture in sufficient quantity.
HARRISON:	The target! The target! You keep moving the target.
EGMONT:	You must disclose on oath the mechanism of your watch and explain to us how duplicates may be constructed. When this is done we will award an amount which, together with monies already advanced, will total £10,000.
HARRISON:	*Ten* thousand? The prize is for twenty. The Act of Queen Anne states clearly –
EGMONT:	The remaining £10,000 can only be paid on proof being made to the satisfaction of this Board that the construction of your timekeeper will provide a method of common and general utility in finding the longitude at sea.
WILLIAM:	What in God's name does such gibberish mean?
MASKELYNE:	It is perfectly clear, Mr Harrison.
WILLIAM:	No it is not perfectly clear, Mr Harrison. 'Provide a method of common and general

utility in finding the longitude at sea'? My father has provided such a method – his timekeeper. It has made two sea voyages and each time has proven accurate to within seconds. What more do you want?

MORTON: We've told you, man. We keep telling you. We need to know *how* it works and we need to assure ourselves it is not too complicated to be reproduced.

HARRISON: Grant me my just prize, and I will refine the watch to make it so.

MORTON: We go round in circles. Let's call this meeting to an end.

HARRISON: It *can* be reproduced! I'm telling you! It can be! Will *no* one listen to me? Is everyone a nincompoop?

EGMONT: Mister Harrison! Sir! Curtail your rudeness and answer me this – can any seaman purchase your invention as an aid to navigation?

HARRISON: Of course not! The machine has only just been invented for God's sake.

EGMONT: Correct! Just so! And therefore we need to spend time satisfying ourselves it can be reproduced. Extraordinary though the Barbados trial was we need to reassure ourselves that it was not owing to chance.

HARRISON: Chance? Do I hear you right? Chance? Have you no understanding of the simplest mechanism? Does the wheel turn without collapsing by 'chance'? Does the arch not cave in by 'chance'? Do your buildings stand erect by 'chance'? Laws govern the movement and structure of things. My timekeeper kept time because it was constructed according to the laws of motion and balance and the laws applying to hot and cold. Even your elusive moon keeps its distance because of laws of gravity – or do you imagine it's a button on God's jacket which he might chance to pull off in a fit of pique?

MORTON: I think, gentlemen, we have an impasse.

HARRISON *and* WILLIAM *return to*

Red Lion Square

ELIZABETH *is polishing her husband's boots. He takes them from her.*

HARRISON: How many times have I told you – I'll polish my own boots.
ELIZABETH: Has he rubbed them up the wrong way again?
WILLIAM: We both did, mother.
ELIZABETH: He gets in the way of himself.
HARRISON: Can't they see ahead?
ELIZABETH: They would see more if you were less bullish.
HARRISON: I'm not bullish, I'm just right.
ELIZABETH: Of course you're right, John. You're just the wrong person to be right.

The Admiralty *meeting continues.*

HARRISON *'barracks'.*

MASKELYNE: And now, gentlemen, I would like to remind the Board of the very persuasive evidence I presented to the honourable members from my recent voyage to the West Indies. I was able to predict the longitude of Barbados to within one half degree, and, on my return,

ACT ONE

> to forecast the longitude of the Isle of Wight to within ten miles of its true position – both by means of the lunars.

HARRISON: The lunars! Hurrah – the lunars!

MASKELYNE: In a very short time I will produce nautical tables –

HARRISON: Nautical headaches.

MASKELYNE: – purchasable for mere pounds rather than the hundreds a watch will cost. And –

HARRISON: And listen. There's more.

MASKELYNE: And finally I would like to recommend that we propose John Harrison be elected a Fellow of the Royal Society.

HARRISON: Confer honours and withhold the prize! How's that for deviousness?

MASKELYNE: Thank you, my Lords.

Exits.

ELIZABETH: What's devious about honours?

HARRISON: Confer honours and silence the noise mongers.

ELIZABETH: That's perverse reasoning, John, and I hope you told them 'yes'.

HARRISON: I told them – not me.

ELIZABETH: You told them 'no'?

HARRISON: What about my son instead, I told them?

Pause.

You'll accept it won't you, William?

WILLIAM: Of course I will, father.

HARRISON: And the silence they intend they won't achieve, right, son?

WILLIAM: Father, they've already achieved what they want to achieve.

Resigned silence.

We must do it.

HARRISON: I know.
WILLIAM: And when you receive the first ten thousand you must hand over all four timekeepers.
HARRISON: I know, I know.
ELIZABETH: You've unleashed their spites.
WILLIAM: And for the remaining £10,000 father must make two more watches, which again must needs be tested at sea.
HARRISON: To prove what?
ELIZABETH: They're asking no more than that you dismantle your timekeeper and demonstrate what you claim, John.
HARRISON: How much more do I have to give, how much longer to fight?
WILLIAM: I'll talk for us, father.
HARRISON: You'd better, my son. Thee must take over. I'm too old to stand before nitwits and explain the perfectness of my watch and argue my case and defend my rights. When a right is so obviously a right I can't find words to say why it's right. I'm contemptuous where I should be patient and arrogant where I should be humble, I know it. But I can do nothing about it. Thee must take over, William, and be the wise mouthpiece for your father.
WILLIAM: Be father to the son's father?
HARRISON: Aye, that.
WILLIAM: Slap his wrists, scold his sins?
HARRISON: Aye, that and that.
WILLIAM: Tell him to be quiet, urge him to hold back, suggest he thinks twice before putting pen to paper to make the world see the world as he sees the world?
HARRISON: Aye, you can try that, too.

WILLIAM *takes his father in his arms.*

WILLIAM: Comfort him in bleak times?

Hold.

HARRISON: [*pushing him away*] As long as tha doesn't sing to me. Tha's not got a right note in thy throat. Since childhood tha's chased notes like butterflies, never quite able to grasp one and hold it.

WILLIAM: So you'll make known the construction of the watch?

HARRISON: Aye, I will.

WILLIAM: Good, father.

Long pause.

HARRISON: On conditions.

ELIZABETH *groans.*

Admiralty

WILLIAM *addresses the Board members –* MORTON, EGMONT *and* MASKELYNE.

HARRISON *in attendance.*

WILLIAM: My father proposes, if it is acceptable to the honourable gentlemen, to explain the mechanism of his watch by handing over the drawings from which it is made together with his explanations in writing –

MORTON: [*viciously interrupting*] No, sir. Not good enough, sir. Not acceptable at all. Yes, your father must hand over the drawings and written explanations, but he must also dismantle the watch in front of the Board's rep-

	resentatives and must answer on oath any questions put to him
HARRISON:	Hark them! I must this and I must that. I hear you talk of 'musts' but do I hear you talk of needs? Of the nation's needs? I hear you talk of 'musts' but do I hear you talk of concerns? Concern for sailors lost at sea along with untold wealth all sunk to Davy's bosom? No – just Harrison must do as he's told. Well Harrison won't, and you can all rot in hell for your damned dishonesty.

FATHER *and* SON *leave.*

EGMONT:	I think we can assume that there's an end to the matter.
MASKELYNE:	No, Lord Egmont. We are dealing with a stubborn man but not a stupid one. He wants the prize, and if we remain firm in our resolve that he reveals the mechanism of his watch to the world I believe he will relent.
EGMONT:	However, I confess sympathy for Harrison's fear of pirating. May I propose that every member of the committee we select to hear the disclosures of the watch's mechanism be enjoined not to disclose them to any but the Board?
MORTON:	Agreed! But let me be honest – I dislike the man. Uncouth. The manners of a pig. No sense of his place –
EGMONT:	Because, Morton, he senses his place to be among the great scientists of the land.
MORTON:	The presumptions of the uneducated! What do you propose, Maskelyne?
MASKELYNE:	He imagines we will relent. We must find a way to let him know unequivocally that we

will not. The man is impressed with the power of print, and so –

Clanging bell.

– I propose we print the minutes of all the meetings of May and June stating our position as well as John Harrison's so that the public can know –

Announcement Platform

COMMISSIONER: [*reading*] '– that it is the opinion of this Board that the terms which have been proposed to Mr Harrison for the discovery of the principles and construction of his timekeeper are reasonable and proper; and that, as he has so peremptorily refused to comply therewith, they do not think themselves authorised to give him any certificate, or that it is to any purpose to treat with him any further on the matter till he alters his present sentiments.'

Sounds as at beginning:

A ticking clock.
A growing storm.
Timber shattering on rock.
Human voices in distress.
Slow dimming of light.

ELIZABETH: [*The Litany*] The *Newcastle*, ninety-six lives lost. Cloves, cardamom, saffron, ginger. The *Doddington*, seventy-six lives lost. Bamboo reeds, elephants' tusks, mother of pearl shells, opium . . .

END OF ACT ONE

ACT TWO

Bustle. Music. Street cries.

Harrison's Workshop

WILLIAM: I think they have us, father.
HARRISON: Schemers!
WILLIAM: I think we must sign the oath.
HARRISON: Must must must!

> *Projections one after the other of Harrison's drawings for the watch. We marvel at the incredible draughtsmanship. The final projection is of the watch itself.*
>
> *The SEVEN NOMINATED MEN gathered round a table studying drawings we see projected.*

ELIZABETH: So sign the oath they did, resentfully; and take his watch to pieces they did, angrily; and explain the mechanism they did arrogantly, cockily – [*Beat.*] – proudly.

> *Throughout, the SEVEN are frozen until –*
>
> *Clanging bell.*

Announcement Platform

COMMISSIONER: [*reading*] 'We whose names are hereunto subscribed do certify that Mr John Harrison has taken his timekeeper to pieces in the presence of us, and explained the principles and construction thereof and that we have compared the drawings of the same with the parts, and do find that they do perfectly correspond.'

Red Lion Square

> HARRISON *sitting for his portrait by* THOMAS KING.

ELIZABETH: Hip hip hooray! Another declaration of approval.

HARRISON: We collect approvals, wife, but no silver.

ELIZABETH: 'Wife'? 'Wife'? What happened to Lizzie? Where's she?

> *Pause.*

Look at him – my uneducated genius from up north. Relax your face, husband. Don't look so stern for those to come.

HARRISON: 'Husband'? You calling me 'husband'?

ELIZABETH: As you're calling me 'wife'.

HARRISON: 'Cos wife you are.

ELIZABETH: As husband *you* are. [*to* KING] Marriage! Beware! From love and wild nights in the loft to dried up indifference. Haranguing is all he cares about these days.

Admiralty

> BOARD MEMBERS *in attendance.*
>
> HARRISON *harangues from his portrait sitting.*

MASKELYNE: Gentlemen of the Board, I must bring to your attention other problems to do with the Harrison timekeeper. Reverend Ludlam, please.

HARRISON: More bloody reverends, more bloody problems!

LUDLAM: Good sirs. As you know, I was one of the seven scientists nominated to receive John Harrison's disclosures of his watch.

HARRISON: Of which they understood little you can be sure.

LUDLAM: Let me say from the outset that our doubts have nothing to do with the candour and proud delight with which this engineering genius dismantled and revealed his machine. There can be no doubt that, however cantankerous –

HARRISON: Cantankerous, that's me!

LUDLAM: – and we all know how the best minds range from the eccentric to the cantankerous – however cantankerous, our carpenter and joiner from the backwaters of Lincolnshire is *more* than a carpenter and joiner. He is an extraordinary, sharp-minded and original inventor.

ELIZABETH: Approvals, John, more approvals! No need to be stern, see!

HARRISON: Wait! They're not done yet.

LUDLAM: No, our misgivings are not only to do with the questionable efficiency of some of the devices fitted to the watch –

HARRISON: I knew I shouldn't have explained anything to them. They don't understand how the bloody wheel works!

LUDLAM: – but with doubts that satisfactory copies can be made by other workmen using everyday methods.

HARRISON: Targets! Targets! They're shifting the targets again.

LUDLAM: Mr Harrison outlined his improvements but could offer no rules for arriving at those

	improvements. He says he adjusted the parts by repeated trials, and that he knows no other method.
HARRISON:	Of course I adjusted the parts by repeated trials. But having done it once I can do it next time with fewer trials. And next time with even fewer trials. And then with no trials at all. It's called 'experience'.
LUDLAM:	Now it may be that such experience can be gained by other workmen but this means that it will be some time before many such watches can be constructed with the same degree of accuracy as that obtained under Mr Harrison's capable hands.
MASKELYNE:	Nevertheless – I move that we authorise Mr Harrison to apply for the first £10,000 – or to be more exact, £7500 since £2500 was allocated him at the conclusion of the first trial to Jamaica.
HARRISON:	Authorise? They authorised what was mine by right, and even then it took another six weeks before I got my money.
ELIZABETH:	But you got it, John. Be fair.
HARRISON:	Fair! Fair! Only half the prize – fair? And look what must I do in return – construct another two. *And* without the original or the drawings to help me! And where *are* the drawings? The scrupulous Reverend Maskelyne wants them, him with three chins and no hair. And to do what? To have them copied and sold to the public, that's what. Said it was now theirs, they'd paid £10,000 for it.
ELIZABETH:	Forgive me saying, Mr Harrison – [*to* KING] I have to challenge him now and then to

	keep him alert – forgive me, Mr Harrison, but £10,000 *is* a lot of money.
HARRISON:	My timekeeper has fulfilled all the requirements for the *full* amount of money.
ELIZABETH:	Good God, man. There is no pleasing you.
HARRISON:	Oh yes there is. Justice pleases me. And honesty. And straight dealing and hard work and rewards for hard work, and what's good for mankind and my fellow creatures – that pleases me. And my timekeeper pleases me.
ELIZABETH:	You will have the last word.
HARRISON:	Nay! *You* will.

At which both laugh.

He kisses her.

ELIZABETH: Why look! A glimmer of past times.

The streets come alive.

Bustle. Music. Street cries.

Red Lion Square

HARRISON *is dictating a letter to his son.*

HARRISON: '. . . and in return for the sum of £800 I will construct two duplicates of the watch, which will become the property of the nation, on condition that at the same time as I be given the £800 I humbly beg the Board to allow me to claim the second award of £10,000, which I would swear on oath would be devoted to the setting up of a manufactory in which workmen and apprentices would be instructed by myself in the construction of further watches for this is the only way my invention will go into the world. And so I humbly urge that my watch be returned to me in order to facilitate production.'

There! What could be fairer than that? More than fair – what could be more practical? Can they deny me that?

Clanging bell.

Can they possibly have arguments against that?

Announcement Platform

COMMISSIONER: [*reading*] '26 April 1766. As Secretary of the Board I am instructed to acquaint you with the following decisions in regard to Mr John Harrison and his proposals as outlined in his letter of the 25th March. That *if* there is any neglect in the prosecution of his invention it is his own. And that only when he shall have made other timekeepers of the same kind as the watch now in possession of the Board, and when such timekeepers have been proven at sea only then will he be entitled to the remaining £10,000.'

WILLIAM: Rejected!

COMMISSIONER: [*continues reading*] 'It is further proposed that because certain members of the Board fear that the undeniably impressive results of the Barbados trial might be a fluke of circumstance, the watch should be sent to the Royal Observatory at Greenwich and there be given rigorous tests over a period of ten months under the personal supervision of the Astronomer Royal, the Reverend Nevil Maskelyne.'

WILLIAM: You're a thorn in their side, father.

HARRISON: Nothing will please them but my death. Well die I won't. I'll hell not die. I know all about them as glory in the end of things, the passing of this and that. *He's* had his day, they say with sadness in their voice and glee in their dried up hearts. Expect no more from him. His days are ended, done! Well pass I won't and end I won't and more there is, and they can *choke* with glee for I've got oak and God and cleverness where they've got naught but three chins and a shiny arse. Oh, yes, I know such men. Beware of them, William lad. They'll drain joy from a nightingale, dampen your sun, and lay waste the best in you. But not in this carpenter, not in this clockmaker, not in this bell-ringer. Don't ask from whence but I've got energies and fires in me to last ten lives and ring them all to hell.

The streets come alive.

Bustle. Music. Street cries.

Red Lion Square

MASKELYNE *arrives.*

MASKELYNE: Mr Harrison.
HARRISON: You, sir!
MASKELYNE: I have a letter for you from the Board.

HARRISON accepts it.

You have been required to deliver up the three machines or timekeepers, now remain-

HARRISON: ing in your hands, which are become the property of the public.

HARRISON: They could find no one else to come for them?

MASKELYNE: Mr Harrison, permit me to remind you that the Royal Observatory was founded for the express purpose of finding longitude by lunar observation –

HARRISON: Did they send you to lecture me, too?

MASKELYNE: – but since becoming Astronomer Royal, to show my impartiality, I have fostered timekeepers no less than I have attended to the motions of the moon. And further –

HARRISON: Spare me!

MASKELYNE: – and further, I know you see me as the demon in your life but I assure you as I assured your son in Barbados – I have been a man of science all my life and what matters to me are my integrity and scientific truth.

HARRISON: While what matters to me is that I have spent thirty years of *my* life engineering these three clocks. What matters to me is that they were never entered for the longitude prize yet they must leave my sight is what matters to me.

MASKELYNE: To which you agreed, let it not be forgotten.

HARRISON: Forgotten is what I most certainly will not let it be, and shall hold you responsible till I die for prevarications, delays and the barriers put before me.

MASKELYNE: Come, Mr Harrison, you exaggerate.

HARRISON: Oh I do, do I? Exaggerate do I? Shall I list them all, those barriers and delays?

MASKELYNE: Sir! The problem of longitude is central to the nation's prosperity, the prize of

£20,000 is a vast sum. And the task of recognising the solution and deciding who has won such a vast sum is a solemn task, and the men chosen to supervise that task are solemn men. What you call barriers we call caution; what you call prevarication we call investigation; what you say is delay we name as trial. Caution, trial and investigation are what an honest nation requires of its honest guardians. Now sir, inform me how best we may carry your precious cargo to the Greenwich Observatory.

HARRISON: First I shall need a receipt for them.
MASKELYNE: Of course. You shall have it.
HARRISON: And it must state they're in perfect order.
MASKELYNE: That I cannot do sir.
HARRISON: Why not, sir? For they are, sir.
MASKELYNE: I'm not able to judge that to be the case.
HARRISON: You don't have to. I'm telling you.
MASKELYNE: If I am to say so then I must know so.
HARRISON: Then you must look at them so, and watch their movements so, and see how like clockwork my clocks go so.
MASKELYNE: And what if when they arrive at the Observatory they function differently from when they were here?
HARRISON: Then you can be sure damage was done on the way, sir.
MASKELYNE: You are an impossible man to deal with, Mr Harrison, do you know that?
HARRISON: No sir, I don't know that.
MASKELYNE: Well I'm telling you that.
HARRISON: And that you tell me that, I should accept that? Is that what that 'that' is about?

MASKELYNE: I really can't stand here battling words with you, sir. I am, let me remind you –

HARRISON: – the Astronomer Royal. I know it. The Very Reverend Astronomer Royal who can't tell if a clock works because his head skips in the clouds with the moon and the stars.

MASKELYNE: Enough, Mr Harrison.

HARRISON: No, not enough, Reverend Maskelyne, sir. Never enough.

MASKELYNE: We must arrive at a wording acceptable to us both.

HARRISON: Till my last days it won't be enough.

MASKELYNE: I propose the following: 'The timekeepers were by appearances in order.'

HARRISON: 'The timekeepers were by *all* appearances in order.'

MASKELYNE: I accept.

HARRISON: 'The timekeepers were by all appearances in *perfect* order.'

MASKELYNE: I accept, I accept. Now, your advice on how to transport them.

HARRISON: Oh, no, sir. You don't catch me like that. I'll not be trapped in giving advice for their transport, for if they be found damaged the blame will be mine.

MASKELYNE: Mr Harrison, this is perverse in the extreme.

HARRISON: Not so. The Board has empowered you to transport my timekeepers, then it must be you who instructs his men how to do so.

MASKELYNE: This is childish.

HARRISON: Childish? Did *I* want them gone?

MASKELYNE: Childish and petulant.

HARRISON: Oh deary me. Childish and petulant.

MASKELYNE: You do not endear yourself to the world, Mr Harrison.

HARRISON: The truth of things needs no endearings, reverend sir, though I know it be the way of your world.
MASKELYNE: Do you want your darlings cared for?
HARRISON: Indeed I do.
MASKELYNE: Then instruct us for heaven's sake.
HARRISON: And be blamed when all goes wrong?
MASKELYNE: You will not be blamed, I vow.
HARRISON: Vow on.
MASKELYNE: I will take full responsibility.
HARRISON: Vow on, vow on!
MASKELYNE: [*furious*] I will vow no more, talk no more, quarrel no more. You will respect, through me, the Board set up by Parliament or I will advise the Board no further dealings with –
HARRISON: [*interrupting*] Then do this. Take Clocks One and Two in pieces. Even you, sir, with your head on the moon will find the sections identifiable. But Clock Three can be moved in one piece. And that's all I have to say to this meeting that was both unannounced and uninvited. Good day, sir.

HARRISON leaves for his workshop.

MASKELYNE nods to TWO WORKMEN *standing by. Between them they lift Clock One. After a few steps it slips out of the hands of one of them and cracks to the ground.*

An electrifying moment.

The streets come alive.

Bustle. Music. Street cries.

ELIZABETH: [*over the bustle*] And on the way out they dropped Clock One and broke some of the movements! But that was not the half of it. The man was so determined to put John out of the race that all three machines were transported to the boat waiting on the Thames not in a chairman's horse – a frame in which all fragile articles are transported – but in an unsprung cart. An unsprung cart! On the cobbled streets! Imagine!

> *A chairman's horse moves across the stage as the clocks are bundled onto an unsprung cart. We watch with horror as they are bounced along.*

And that man was entrusted with John's life and our future!

Admiralty

MASKELYNE, HARRISON, WILLIAM, EGMONT *and* MORTON.

MASKELYNE: Gentlemen, the Board of Longitude laid down very detailed instructions for the ten-month trial of the watch which I conducted. All actions were to be witnessed by retired officers of the Royal Greenwich Hospital –

ELIZABETH: – who were decrepit old naval cast-offs unable to see what they're witnessing – those that could climb the hill, that is.

MASKELYNE: I was to keep daily records which the Commissioners authorised me to make public.

ELIZABETH: And what a record of lies they were.

MASKELYNE: My summing up was fair and just. I divided the ten months into seven hypothetical sea voyages of six weeks each, and for each except the last, the errors were of such variation as not to warrant the Queen Anne Prize.

HARRISON: Not our errors, reverend sir. Your distortions.

MASKELYNE: I concluded that Mr Harrison's watch cannot be depended upon to keep the longitude within a degree in a West India voyage of six weeks. Nevertheless, this fourth of his timepieces is a useful and valuable invention, and –

ELIZABETH: Wait! Here it comes!

MASKELYNE: – and in conjunction with lunar observations may be of considerable advantage to navigation.

HARRISON: Humbug! If my watch can't be depended upon to keep the longitude then how can it be 'of considerable advantage to navigation'? Humbug! Hypocrite!

MORTON: Mr Harrison, sir, I will not have you constantly impugning the Astronomer Royal's integrity.

HARRISON: [*to his son*] You explain it to them, William. I'm tired.

WILLIAM: It is too complicated, father. These are laymen.

HARRISON: Professors and priests, I know. Try!

WILLIAM: [*trying*] No clock runs accurately to the split second.

MORTON: Don't tell us what we already know!

WILLIAM: All clocks gain or lose seconds each day. If it loses or gains erratically –

MORTON: Nor do I want to be spoken to like a child.

WILLIAM: I must tell you what you know in preparation for what you don't know. If the watch loses or gains erratically then it becomes impossible to gauge longitude. If, on the other hand, it loses or gains the same or similar amounts each day then an average daily allowance can be made in the calculating of longitude. Reverend Maskelyne failed to make such an allowance during his ten-month trial of our timepiece.

MASKELYNE: The rate was too irregular.

WILLIAM: The rate was irregular when the watch was laid down on its back –

MASKELYNE: Which is what the Board stipulated.

WILLIAM: No, sir. The Board stipulated that the trials should be for the watch lying at different angles.

MASKELYNE: And that I did, too, sir.

WILLIAM: But for only the last forty-five days in the ten-month trial.

MASKELYNE: And recorded the results fairly.

WILLIAM: But you did not calculate the *entire* ten months making any allowance for gain.

MASKELYNE: The gains were too various.

WILLIAM: Not according to your own records they weren't. According to your own records you should have applied a gain of 19.51 in all your calculations.

MASKELYNE: I could not imagine you would want that when on your trip to Barbados you requested a gaining rate of only one second a day to be allowed.

WILLIAM: Had you spoken to us first we'd have told you that we'd not yet adjusted the watch satisfactorily.

MASKELYNE: And whose fault was that?

WILLIAM: We were not given time or opportunity.

EGMONT: Because everyone was so heartily sick of the quarrels that erupted whenever you were around.

MORTON: And had father and son not sulked they could have sent word that the watch was not in a perfect state.

WILLIAM: You might have guessed the watch could not be in a perfect state after it had been taken apart.

HARRISON: Should've taken the reverend apart, see how well he functioned after being reassembled.

WILLIAM: And had you applied the gaining rate of 19.51 seconds overall, then hypothetical voyage one and hypothetical voyage four would each have won us £20,000.

HARRISON: What do you say to that?

MASKELYNE: I say to that that I will print my report and let the world know what's what.

HARRISON: And to that I say I, too, will let the world know what's what.

MASKELYNE: And what, precisely, *is* it that you'll let the world know?

HARRISON: How the Board behaved illegally, that is what I'll let the world know.

MORTON: Damn it, Mr Harrison, I won't have the Board insulted in this way.

HARRISON: Then deny it.

MORTON: Deny what, precisely? Precisely how did the Board behave illegally?

HARRISON: You allowed my devices to be publicly exposed when you swore they would be kept private.

MASKELYNE: It didn't matter! Your beautiful watch was too complicated for your contemporaries to copy, anyway.

EGMONT: And you have shown us no plans for other watches.

HARRISON: A fifth watch is in construction!

WILLIAM: – which of course you will now want on trial at the Royal Observatory for the space of another ten successive months –

HARRISON: – another ten months to wait –

WILLIAM: You keep changing the rules.

HARRISON: Another trial!

WILLIAM: You keep changing the bloody rules!

HARRISON: And look! You've made my son swear!

The streets come alive.

Bustle. Music. Street cries.

ELIZABETH: And so, the Board, fearing that no one but my John could replicate his watch, commissioned the famous clockmaker, Larcum Kendall, to do so for the sum of £450.

WILLIAM: And beautifully made it was. Very fine.

Admiralty

MASKELYNE, EGMONT, MORTON *and* KENDALL.

MASKELYNE: Gentlemen. We have subjected Mr Kendall's replica of the Harrison watch to the same tests, and now they've proved satisfactory we've asked Mr Kendall to tell us the terms under which he would instruct other workmen to make further copies.

KENDALL: And I must decline so to do, sirs. In my view the Board will be disappointed to rely on watches like the Harrison watch ever coming into general use at sea unless the expensive parts of the watch can be reduced in costs and a simpler method be contrived to adjust the mechanism.

EGMONT: Can you construct such a watch?
KENDALL: I can, my Lord.
EGMONT: Leaving out the *expensive* parts?
KENDALL: I can, my Lord.
EGMONT: Making the adjustments *simpler*?
KENDALL: All that, my Lord, and thus they will come into general use at sea.
EGMONT: Thank you, Mr Kendall.
KENDALL: Thank you, my Lords.

He leaves.

MORTON: Let the man do it, I say.
EGMONT: It's not so easy, Morton. The King George Act protects the Harrisons.
MORTON: Criminal mistake if you ask me. Look at the difference in time. The Harrisons have been working on their fifth watch for four years while Kendall here produced his in two and a half.
EGMONT: How if we were to ask Parliament to legislate that Harrison forfeits his rights to the second £10,000 unless his two remaining watches are completed within five years?
MORTON: That'll send him into print again!

Bring in Red Lion Square

HARRISON: They can laugh and scoff all they want – it only further proves what damned rapscallions they are. That prize is mine! The Barbados trial proved it and the world knows it!
MORTON: The world also knows the damned watch has to do more than function at sea – it has

EGMONT: to be manufacturable so that every damned seaman can purchase the damn thing.

EGMONT: And Kendall can solve the problem but we can't ask him to because we're tied to the Harrisons by old legislation.

HARRISON: Ungrateful bastards!

MORTON: And he calls us ungrateful. Ungrateful? John Harrison – *that's* who's ungrateful. In four years he's produced no new watches, and the legislation we're proposing gives him another five for God's sake.

HARRISON: By which time I'll be eighty-two!

MORTON: And if by then nothing is produced then it never will be, and he'll have earned from the nation £10,000 and a luxurious old age, the old battleaxe! I never liked the man.

The street comes alive.

Bustle. Music. Street cries.

Red Lion Square

HARRISON: But we beat them. Ha! Ha! The rapscallions! Ho! Ho! Parliament wouldn't *pass* the legislation they wanted, and I've finished my new watch! A fifth timepiece! *And* simpler! *And* cheaper! Bloody lovely! Bloody ingenious. Bloody, bloody, bloody serves them right. I've done it.

WILLIAM: Only half true, father. Done it all bar the final adjustments.

HARRISON: Half truths are not lies, my son, they're just the truth waiting to be completed.

Long, contemplative pause.

WILLIAM:	But you have still to make a sixth timepiece, father.
HARRISON:	I know it.
WILLIAM:	No second ten thousand, else.
HARRISON:	I know it, I know it!
WILLIAM:	The Board stipulated and we agreed – new watches, new tests.
HARRISON:	And the years are passing.
ELIZABETH:	And we don't dance any more, and you don't call me 'my love' any more.
HARRISON:	I can't do it, William.
ELIZABETH:	[*The Litany*] The *Lincoln*, ninety-six lives lost. Cinnamon, cashew nuts, tamarinds, vermilion . . .
HARRISON:	I can't.
WILLIAM:	I know it.
ELIZABETH:	[*The Litany*] The *Resolution*, ninety-nine lives lost. Saltpetre, rice, tigers' teeth, chintz . . .
HARRISON:	Too old, too weary.
ELIZABETH:	Too bitter, my love.
HARRISON:	Fight's gone.
ELIZABETH:	[*The Litany*] The *Phoenix*. Eighty lives lost. Muslins, calicoes, nankeen, sugar candy . . .
WILLIAM:	I have one last thought, father. [*Beat.*] King George. [*Beat.*] A letter to him. I hear he has sympathy for our case.

Richmond Observatory

KING GEORGE III *and* DR DEMAINBRAY, *his Swiss philosophy tutor.*

DEMAINBRAY:	[*reading*] 'Man is only a reed, the weakest in nature, but – he is a *thinking* reed. Even if the universe were to crush him, man would still

be nobler than his slayer, because he knows that he is dying and the advantage the universe has over him. The universe knows none of this. Thus all our dignity consists in thought.' Who said this?

GEORGE: I know who should have said it.

DEMAINBRAY: Who?

GEORGE: Me! I should have said it 'cos then I'd be a wise king. [*Beat.*] Pascal.

DEMAINBRAY: I'm impressed, sire.

GEORGE: You should be. It's why I engaged you as my tutor. Not simply to teach me philosophy but to be impressed by me and keep telling me you're impressed by me.

DEMAINBRAY: Died young, Pascal.

GEORGE: I like clever young men. The future of the nation.

DEMAINBRAY: What about clever old ones, sire?

GEORGE: The Harrison saga. Not good. Not good at all. Not just. And as for my Lords Morton and Egmont – well, I'm not sure what *they're* going to bequeath the nation.

DEMAINBRAY: Egmont is charming, eccentric.

GEORGE: But dissipated. He'll be dead in a trice.

DEMAINBRAY: Morton is a clever astronomer.

GEORGE: But a tight-arsed amateur, and we all know what bullies tight-arsed amateurs are. The Harrison letter says they had a good relationship with the Board –

DEMAINBRAY: – friendly, helpful –

GEORGE: – up until the trial of the timepiece to Jamaica –

DEMAINBRAY: – which was a success –

GEORGE: – but after which, the help and friendliness disappeared, and now we – what?

DEMAINBRAY: [*reading*] '– and now we find ourselves browbeaten by one set of men and betrayed by another.'

GEORGE: Not good. Not good at all. These people have been badly treated. Read me their last paragraph again.

DEMAINBRAY: [*reading*] 'If His Majesty would be so graciously pleased to suffer our new made watch, to be lodged for a certain time in the Observatory at Richmond, in order to ascertain and manifest its degree of excellence, I should hope that the prejudices of many might thereby be vanquished, and that it would be easy to obtain redress.'

GEORGE: We'll do it. A six-week trial of the new watch, Dr Demainbray. By God, Harrison, I will see you righted.

DEMAINBRAY: Here, in your own observatory, sire?

GEORGE: Of course here, of course. Where else? I shall enjoy that. I'm getting excited just thinking about it.

The streets come alive.

Bustle. Music. Street cries.

GEORGE III, DEMAINBRAY *and* WILLIAM *confront the box.*

GEORGE: Now, gentlemen, the procedure is simple. Like the other tests. To ensure the fifth Harrison watch won't be tampered with I've had three locks fitted to the outer box here containing the watch. I'll hold one key, Dr Demainbray a second, and you, Mr Harrison, the third. We'll meet here every day at noon, check the temperature, check the watch with the regulator clock, and rewind it. The good doctor will keep a record, which we'll each initial, and in the end we'll see what's what and who's who and the next to be done. Oh, I am *so* excited.

The THREE MEN *separate.*

The bustling street takes over.

The MEN *come together again. Three locks unlocked. Times compared.*

GEORGE: Well! What do we say to this? Your timekeeper is so different from the regulator clock it's not good from here to the city, never mind from Portsmouth to Barbados.

DEMAINBRAY: Perhaps the watch needs to settle, sire.

WILLIAM: Shouldn't need settling. Should be going from the start.

GEORGE: We'll give it a few days.

The THREE MEN *separate.*

The bustling street takes over.

They come together again. Three locks unlocked. Times compared.

GEORGE: Well this is no good, Mr Harrison. Your timekeeper is way out.

WILLIAM: I don't understand it, sire. I'm looking and looking and can see nothing to cause such erratic behaviour.

GEORGE: Right! We'll lock it up, then. Try again tomorrow, then.

The THREE MEN *separate.*

The bustling street takes over.

They come together again with much trepidation.

GEORGE: I'm almost frightened to unlock the wretched thing. I do have a reputation to think of, Harrison. I hope you and your father aren't going to let me down?

They unlock the case.

Check the time.

GEORGE: Out! Out again!
WILLIAM: I'm at a loss, sire. I can only assure you there is absolutely no reason, no reason at all why this watch shouldn't function.
GEORGE: Demainbray?
DEMAINBRAY: I'm astounded. I have every faith in John Harrison's skills but –
WILLIAM: I ask for a full week, sire. And then I'll take it back to my father who is so distressed, *so* distressed it can't be imagined.
GEORGE: Oh yes it can! I'm also feeling sick and anxious – for whom more I can't tell, your father or myself. *You* don't look too good, either, young Harrison. Rewind it, sir, and we'll be on our ways.

As WILLIAM *winds.*

I've got all these dratted children to play father to. I don't know what's wrong with Charlotte. She keeps having these babies. And they all turn out to be cleverer than me by the age of five. I couldn't read till the age of eleven you know. Did you know that? Now I've got Demainbray here to talk philosophy to me. Keep me sharp, so's I can answer back my ten-year-old. You done?

WILLIAM: Wound, sir.

GEORGE: Don't look so glum, man. All's for the best in this best of all possible worlds. Or is that inappropriate, Demainbray?

DEMAINBRAY: Excellent, sire, excellent! I'm impressed.

They separate.

But before they're apart GEORGE *cries out.*

GEORGE: Oh ye Gods and little fishes! The cupboard! The cupboard!

The other two are mesmerised by his agitation.

He throws open the cupboard and retrieves three small rocks.

Lodestones! Of course your watch wouldn't function. Powerful magnetic lodestones! Using them for my own daft experiments. Pulling your timekeeper all over the place. Scatterbrain! Cretin! Run home, William. Tell your father. We'll test it for more than six weeks.

WILLIAM: Yes, sir.

GEORGE: We'll test it for eight.

WILLIAM: Yes, sir.

GEORGE: Nay, ten. Nay, twelve weeks to prevent any cavilling. Tell him –

WILLIAM: I will, sir.

GEORGE: His watch will work. Hallelujah!

Handel's triumphant 'Hallelujah Chorus'.

The MEN *separate.*

Street bustle adds to the excitement of the moment.

Dies away.

Red Lion Square

HARRISON: Never did like Mr Handel. The man refused to tune his instruments to suit the voice. Voice went one way, instrument another. Don't much care for Mr Shakespeare, either. Too many thoughts contradicting each other. If my timekeeper is driven by mechanical laws so music and writing must be. Can't abide the ornate. Made the first watch ornate. A mistake. Changed all that with the next watch. Plain. Simple. Practical. To hell with flowery Shakespeare. Less is more. Give me a simple Psalm. 'The Lord is my shepherd, I shall not want.' Practical, simple, plain.

ELIZABETH: But – nothing is plain and simple about my plain and simple husband. Not content with the King's support he commissioned another pamphlet to be written because the other one he wrote couldn't be understood, it had sentences so long you lost your way before meaning could dawn; and this commissioned pamphlet he sent to every member of Parliament: 'The Case Of John Harrison'.

And then came an event we'll remember till our dying day. Unannounced, no warning, the King knocked on our door. George himself!

GEORGE III *appears.*

Comically embarrassed responses from HARRISON *and* ELIZABETH.

I didn't know what to do, bow or curtsey or go down on my knees. I think I did all three. He called for port, stopped us fussing, and made himself at home like an old friend.

Close, intimate, late night atmosphere.

GEORGE: I understand you, Mr Harrison, believe me. But the time for haranguing is past. It has led nowhere and it *will* lead nowhere. Still your anger and listen to me. You think that because the *King* tested your timekeeper the Board must relent and award you the second part of the £20,000 prize. They can't. They've been given a task by Parliament who've made them the sole authority to help find longitude at sea. Any test must be an official one controlled by them. Listen to me. I know the Board – austere men, a bit bloodless, not even the King can go against them, and that, dear man, is the way of the world, which I suspect you and your son have never really understood. Bit unworldly, both of you, if you'll forgive my saying. But – and this, too, is the way of the world, the Board just will not award you more money – they must save face, and we mustn't stop them saving face. Now – Parliament on the other hand can reward achievement. I'll arrange that with the Prime Minister and he will arrange it with the powers that be. Trust me on that.

HARRISON: [*drifting off, quoting*] 'He hath led me and brought me into darkness but not into light. Surely against me is he turned; he turneth his hand against me all the day.'

GEORGE: No, Mr Harrison, sir. No, no, no! The world tires of lamentations – even Jeremiah's. Leave off printing your pamphlets and telling your story over and over again. I urge you. See this ring on my finger – it's a watch. John Arnold made it – a brilliant young watchmaker who has already made two watches for sailors at a fraction of what it has cost you. The Board is no longer interested in your complaints to them. Listen hard to me, Mr Harrison, sir – the young are clamouring for attention. Forget the Board, appeal to the Prime Minister. I'll prepare the way for you.

Church Pews

As HARRISON *returns to his young manhood he intones.*

HARRISON: 'My flesh and my skin hath he made old; he hath broken my bones. He hath set me in dark places as they that be dead of old.'

A YOUNG HARRISON *is now before his* CHOIR OF MEN *in church, who shuffle uncertainly.*

Come on now, you ploughmen. You don't walk backwards when you plough. And you tailors, you don't sew behind your backs. Nor none of you shoemakers, carpenters, smithies, weavers – you don't work not facing your work. So why should you sing with your backs to the congregation? Face them. Stop shuffling and arrange yourselves. Basses in front, tenors in the pews behind, and trebles behind them. We've got strangers today, sing out for them. Sing out.

He conducts. They sing.

Clanging bell.

Against the choral background ELIZABETH *mounts the Announcement Platform.*

ELIZABETH: Listen to this, my curmudgeonly husband. [*reading*] 'Because John Harrison of Red Lion Square, having for forty-eight years applied himself with unremitting industry to the making of a timekeeper for ascertaining the longitude at sea; and having discovered the principles of constructing the same by which other timekeepers have already been made, and from which great benefit will arise to the trade and navigation of these kingdoms, he is highly deserving of public reward. Be it therefore enacted that the Treasurer of His Majesty's navy shall cause to be paid to the said John Harrison a sum not exceeding £8750 . . .'

Red Lion Square

WILLIAM *helps his father from church to his chair at home, which is now centre stage.*

Singing continues.

HARRISON: It should have come from the Board not Parliament.

WILLIAM: No matter, father, it's come.
HARRISON: And it should have been £10,000.
ELIZABETH: Well it wasn't, old man, not unless you add the £4000 you received over forty-eight years.
HARRISON: In which case – ha ha! hee hee! ho ho! – it becomes £22,750.
ELIZABETH: Oh, good God! Will he never relent?
HARRISON: £2750 more than the offered prize!
ELIZABETH: You mischievous old bugger, you.
HARRISON: Still, small consolation for the soured joy of it all.
WILLIAM: Let's console ourselves this way, father. Not merely with the knowledge that we deserved better treatment but with the knowledge that our fame is in the hands of impartial posterity.

HARRISON *is seated.*

HARRISON: I wish, William, upon every father a son like thee.
ELIZABETH: Amen to that.

WILLIAM *leaves.*

Singing still in the background.

Lone irrepressible, unquenchable figure centre stage.

HARRISON: And now – let me treat of another matter that has come my way and must be of worth if rightly thought about as I have done, namely this: because in nature there is no such thing as major or minor tones, therefore as the diameter and radius of a circle is to its circumference, so, too, is the sharp third to the octave. And I have constructed a musical scale based on this principle.

ELIZABETH is at some domestic chore. Polishing a brass tray?

ELIZABETH: What's musical scales got to do with watchmaking you're wondering? Nothing, really, except it was one man thought about both.

HARRISON: The chief consequence of my musical scale is the creation of intervals of melody truly sweet and mathematically perfect in a way never before thought possible.

Next two speeches interwoven – a duet.

ELIZABETH: John Harrison . . .
HARRISON: Away with your nonsensical chromatic and enharmonic scale –
ELIZABETH: . . . carpenter and joiner . . .
HARRISON: – all buzzed and blazed about the world through ignorance.
ELIZABETH: . . . tuner of bells . . .
HARRISON: Only one true scale of music exists –
ELIZABETH: . . . choirmaster . . .
HARRISON: – and it is stupendously obvious –
ELIZABETH: . . . mender of clocks.
HARRISON: – because so well grounded in *my* explanations.
ELIZABETH: Helped change the world.
HARRISON: But who listened?
ELIZABETH: My curmudgeon.
HARRISON: Spite and poison run through malicious minds that object to what is proven and true.
ELIZABETH: My husband.

HARRISON: And neither my musical scales nor my longitude will ever be proven or completed until such minds resign or die.

Singing swells.

ELIZABETH: My curmudgeon, my husband.

HARRISON *rises. The* YOUNG HARRISON *now.*

HARRISON: Sing out you weavers and smithies! Sing out you shoemakers, carpenters, ploughmen and boys.
Sing out!

Singing swells and swells.

END

Street Cries

Pretty maids, pretty pins, pretty women!
Buy a fine singing bird, a fine singing bird.
Buy any wax or wafers? Fine writing ink?
Old shoes for some broomes! Old shoes for some broomes!
Chimney sweep! Chimney sweep!
Old cloaks, old suits, any old coats!
Lilly white vinegar! Vinegar light as Lillies!
Old chairs to mend! Old chairs to mend!
Twelve pence a peck, Oysters. Twelve pence a peck.
Old Satten, Old Taffety, or Velvet!
Buy a new Almanack! Buy a new Almanack!
Buy my singing glasses, singing glasses, buy my singing glasses.
Any kitchen stuff have you, maids? Knives, combs, or inkhorns?
Four for sixpence, Mack-er-el. Four for sixpence, Mack-er-el.
Any work for the Cooper? Cooper, Cooper, any work for the Cooper?
Four pair for a shilling, Holland socks! Holland socks! Four pair for a shilling.
Colly Molly Puffe Pastries, Colly Molly Puffe!
'Ere's yer toys for girls an' boys!
Who's for mutton pie, or an eel pie?
Sand, ho! Buy my nice white sand, ho!
Any new river water, water here?
Fine ripe duke cherries, a ha'penny a stick and a penny a stick, ripe duke cherries!
Shrimps like prawns, a ha'penny a pot!

By the same author

plays

THE WESKER TRILOGY:
(Chicken Soup with Barley, Roots,
I'm Talking About Jerusalem)
The Kitchen
The Four Seasons
Their Very Own and Golden City
Chips with Everything
The Friends
The Old Ones
Love Letters on Blue Paper
The Journalists
The Wedding Feast
Shylock
One More Ride on the Merry-Go-Round
Caritas
When God Wanted a Son
Lady Othello
Bluey
Badenheim 1939
Shoeshine and Little Old Lady (*plays for young people*)
Beorhtel's Hill
Men Die Women Survive
Blood Libel
Wild Spring
Break My Heart
Barabbas
Denial
Longitude
Letter to Myself

short stories
Six Sundays in January
Love Letters on Blue Paper
Said the Old Man to the Young Man
The King's Daughters

essays and non-fiction
Fears of Fragmentation
Distinctions
Say Goodbye, You May Never See Them Again
Journey Into Journalism
As Much As I Dare (autobiography)
The Birth of Shylock and the Death of Zero Mostel

for children
Fatlips

novels
Honey

opera librettos
Caritas
Grief

Chronology of First Performances

Chicken Soup with Barley (Belgrade Theatre, Coventry; then Royal Court) 1958

Roots (Belgrade Theatre, Coventry; then Royal Court) 1959

I'm Talking About Jerusalem (Belgrade Theatre, Coventry; then Royal Court) 1960

The Kitchen (Royal Court) 1961

Chips with Everything (Royal Court; then Vaudeville Theatre) 1962

The Nottingham Captain (Wellingborough Festival) 1962

Menace (BBC TV) 1963

The Four Seasons (Belgrade Theatre, Coventry; then Saville Theatre, London) 1965

Their Very Own and Golden City (Belgium National Theatre; Royal Court, 1966) 1965

The Friends (Stadsteater, Stockholm; Roundhouse) 1970

The Old Ones (Royal Court) 1972

The Wedding Feast (Stadsteater, Stockholm; West Yorkshire Playhouse, Leeds, 1977) 1974

Shylock (The Merchant) (Royal Dramatic Theatre, Stockholm; Birmingham Repertory Theatre, 1978) 1976

Love Letters on Blue Paper (Syracuse Stage, USA; Cottesloe, National Theatre, 1978) 1977

Caritas (Cottesloe, National Theatre) 1981

The Journalists (Stadtstheater, Wilhelmshaven, W. Germany) 1981

Four Portraits – of Mothers (Mitzukoshi Royal Theatre, Tokyo; Edinburgh Festival, 1984) 1982

Annie Wobbler (Birmingham Repertory Theatre; then New End Theatre) 1983

Sullied Hand (Edinburgh Festival) 1984

Yardsale (Edinburgh Festival; Lyric Theatre Studio, 1987) 1985

One More Ride on the Merry-Go-Round (Phoenix Theatre, Leicester) 1985

Bluey (BBC Radio 3) 1985

Whatever Happened to Betty Lemon? (Théâtre du Rond-Point, Paris; Lyric Theatre Studio, 1987) 1986

Beorhtel's Hill (Towngate Theatre, Basildon) 1989

The Mistress (Festival of One-Act Plays, Arezzo; Sherman Theatre, Cardiff, 1997) 1991

Letter to a Daughter (Sanwoolim Theatre Company, Seoul; Edinburgh Festival, Assembly Rooms, 1998) 1992

Men Die Women Survive (Three Women Talking) (Northlight Theater, Chicago) 1992

Wild Spring (Bungaku-za Theatre Company, Tokyo) 1994

Blood Libel (Norwich Playhouse) 1996

When God Wanted a Son (New End Theatre) 1997

Break, My Heart (Sherman Theatre, Cardiff, and HTV) 1997

Barabbas (BBC TV) 2000

Denial (Bristol Old Vic) 2000

The Kitchen Musical (Chijinkai Theatre Company, Tokyo) 2000

Groupie (BBC Radio 4, 2001, then on stage by Company Gli Ipocriti of Naples at Festival di Todi, Italy) 2001

Letter to Myself (Aberystwyth University Studio Theatre) 2004

Longitude (Greenwich Theatre, London) 2005

For more information about the author please visit website www.arnoldwesker.com